C000006722

Windsor and Eton Express
1812-1830
The Charles Knight Years

By Brigitte Mitchell

and members of Windsor Local History Group
Sue Ashley (SA)
Hester Davenport (HD)
Carol Dixon Smith (CDS)
Elias Kupfermann (EK)
Pamela Marson (PM)
Sue Mercer (SM)
Barbara Mitch (BEM)
Norman Oxley (NO)
Sonia Sayed (SS)

WINDSOR LOCAL HISTORY GROUP

The picture on the front cover is a hand tinted engraving of Windsor in 1812. The background is a page of the Windsor Express.

The pictures on the back cover are of the young Charles Knight Senior and Charles Knight Junior in old age, and are reproduced by permission of the Royal Borough of Windsor & Maidenhead Civic Collection. They both hang in the Mayor's Parlour at Windsor Guildhall and can sometimes be viewed as part of a visit to Windsor Museum.

Windsor Local History Publications Group was formed in 1976 from a small group of WEA students and tutors with the aim of fostering research in the field of local history and publishing the results. The name was changed to Windsor Local History Group in 2004.

Officers in 2012
Life President: John Handcock CVO DL
Chairman: Dr Brigitte Mitchell
Secretary: Sue Ashley
Treasurer: Barbara Mitch

Editorial Committee: Brigitte Mitchell, Hester Davenport, Sue Ashley
Photographs and desk top publishing: Pamela Marson
Picture research: Elias Kupfermann

Copyright Windsor Local History Group ©
All right reserved

No part of this publication may be reproduced, stored in a retrieval system, or transmitted in any form or by any means, electronic, mechanical, photocopying, recording or otherwise, without prior permission of the copyright holder.
First Published 2012
Printed in England by Creeds the Printers
ISBN 978 0 9505 5678 9

Contents

George IV by Thomas Lawrence.

This picture was given to Windsor Corporation by the King and is now in Windsor Guildhall. The *Windsor Express* reports that it originally had to be taken in through the window as it is 11 feet by 8 feet. It is reproduced by kind permission of the Royal Borough of Windsor & Maidenhead Civic Collection.

George IV had just become Prince Regent when the *Windsor Express* was first published and died in June 1830. The period covered in this book coincides with his Regency and reign.

4

PREFACE

'Britain is justly proud of the fashion in which her Press behaves and the discretion and judgement usually exercised in every field of criticism' – Sir Gerald Nabarro.

One of life's near impossibilities in the twenty-first century is to keep up, however perfunctorily, one's perusal of the daily papers. In consequence, it can barely be imagined how a team of members of the Windsor Local History Group have conscientiously and effectively perused back numbers of Windsor's own newspaper from 1 August 1812. That they have completed this Homeric task with remarkable success and sensitivity will be manifestly apparent from the reading of the diverse and fascinating chapters of this absorbing book, which concentrates on the first two decades of the paper.

The founders of the *Windsor and Eton Express*, Charles Knight and his son, also Charles, of whom there are illuminating biographical sketches, published their paper for a bare fifteen years before passing on the baton but in that time they established a newspaper whose weekly reports then covered national and international news as well as local stories.

We are vouchsafed a galaxy of glimpses into festivities and floods, health and hostelries, culture and Castle, crime and Courts, revels and Royalty and naturally the garrisons. In this latter piece, we are offered such gems as the officer of the XXIII Light Dragoons riding his horse up the 142 steps of the so-called *Hundred Steps* into the Cloisters of St George's Chapel and the rumbustious welcome afforded to troops returning from the battlefield of Waterloo.

It was said of Professor Sir Albert Richardson that 'He only reads eighteenth-century newspapers for he says the news in them is just the same as it is today. You merely have to substitute the names of countries occasionally.' Applying this assertion to various episodes in the centuries embraced in this informative volume, one sees how history again and again repeats itself. The riots around the country 'sparked by chronic unemployment and high food prices' were mirrored in the country's riots in 2011; the collapse of banks, notably Windsor's Brown and Coombs, were echoed by the twenty-first century failure of Northern Rock and others; the 1814 floods occasioned by a giant freeze and its sudden thaw were exactly replicated in 1947.

For this exemplary book Windsor Local History Group is to be congratulated: it is a valuable and intriguing excursion into our history 200 years ago, seen through the pages of the town's very own newspaper. Although William Pitt was accustomed to declare 'I know how little newspapers can be trusted' perhaps the last word should – at least in this Preface – rest with Richmal Crompton's incomparable William Brown: 'It's in a newspaper so it must be true'. May the impeccable standards of the Charles Knights, father and son, vindicate William's opinion and the *Windsor and Eton Express* continue to serve the local community as valiantly and vigorously as has been the case over the last 200 years.

John E Handcock, CVO, DL
President, WLHG

Castle Street Windsor showing the bookshop from which the first Express was published. John Burgiss Brown became joint proprietor and publisher for a short time and then took over Charles Knight's shop and works

Round the corner from Castle Street (now Castle Hill) showing the entrance to the print shop, where the people are walking. This is now called Market Street, but in 1812 was Queen Street.

The *Windsor and Eton Express* Newspaper

On 1 August 1812 Charles Knight Sr and his son Charles Knight Jr published the first edition of the *Windsor and Eton Express* in their book shop at 2 Castle Hill, Windsor. It was printed at the back of the shop. 200 years later the paper is still going strong. This anniversary volume looks at the early years of the newspaper, the Charles Knight years, from 1812 to 1830, opening a window on a small part of history of Windsor, of England and even the rest of the world.

Before the *Windsor and Eton Express* came into being, there was only one newspaper published in Berkshire, the *Reading Mercury,* founded in 1723. Charles Knight Jr wrote in his autobiography:

> My friend would make the stirring events of the week known to his household in reading aloud the *Reading Mercury* which was duly delivered at his door by an old newsman on a shambling pony. How eagerly we looked for this message.

Even during the early years of the *Express,* papers were delivered on foot or by pony express by special newsmen to local subscribers. They also were responsible for receiving the correct number of papers, and collecting the quarterly accounts. Charles Knight Jr remembers ruefully that the quarterly accounts often grew into half yearly or yearly settlements, which caused him no end of financial problems and finally led him to sell the paper.

What sort of a world was the first Windsor newspaper born into?

1812 was a particularly bleak year. One historian has recently voted it the worst year in British history. The country had been at war with France for 19 years (since 1793), a war that was still dominated by Napoleon's successes in Europe, although he had just embarked on his disastrous Russian campaign.

The British army had recently gained a foothold in Portugal to chase the French out of Spain but the retreat to Corunna with the death of the Commander-in-chief Sir John Moore were still vivid memories. Wellington, who had been brought over from India to replace him in the Peninsular, was facing a large French army near Salamanca.

Across the Atlantic, the USA had declared war on Britain, a trade war, but also a war in support of the French. The economy at home was in dire straits, a disastrous harvest caused bread prices to rise to an alarming 20d per quartern* loaf (about four times the pre war price); the poor were desperate and the Luddites were breaking machinery around the country. In May Spencer Percival, the Prime Minister, had been assassinated; it could not get any worse.

Charles Knight Jr admitted that 'the political atmosphere was not very bright on the 1 August 1812, when the Windsor newspaper struggled into life'.

The early part of the century saw a series of poor harvests and bitter cold winters, which were reflected in the high price of bread. Much of the distress around the country is reported in the newspaper, and yet you do not get the feeling of despair or doom. But good news **was** just beginning to filter through from the war; the second week of publication carries the news of Wellington's victory at Salamanca and of the general rejoicing around the country.

Then there were of course the wars and trade embargos and the Corn Laws, and after the French wars thousands of discharged soldiers flooded the labour market but could not find work. All this and more we can find reported in the early years of the newspaper together with suggestions on how to employ the unemployed. But there were also entertainments, the theatre and revels on Bachelors' Acre. Charles Knight Jr sold the paper in 1827, but was still using it to advertise his books. We have continued to 1830, the death of George IV, and the beginning of serious discussions about Parliamentary reform.

* See 'The Price of Bread'

What did this newspaper look like?

The *Windsor and Eton Express and General Advertiser for Berks, Bucks, Middlesex, Surrey, Herts, Oxon, Hants and Wilts,* was ambitiously titled, given the limitations on transport of the day. Indeed the flat-bed hand printing presses could only deal with 200-250 news-sheets per hour.

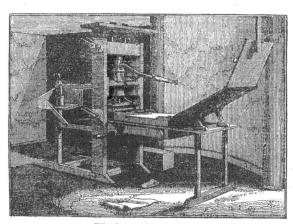

[The Common Printing Press.]

What is surprising also is the cost of the newspaper, 6½d shortly to go up to 7d, which put it beyond the means of a working man. It was the stamp duty that dictated the high price of newspapers of the time. Stamp duty was lowered in 1836 from 4d per paper to 1d, and abolished altogether in 1855, creating the cheap popular press Charles Knight Jr had fought for all his life.

What is difficult for the modern reader, is that there are almost no headlines and different news-items follow each other by just starting a new paragraph.

The first page consisted of advertising, notices and property sales. Fire insurance predominated in the early years. There was also a weekly state lottery with a maximum win of £80,000. Lotteries run by private concerns competed with the state lottery. But ticket prices from £7 to £18 put it out of the reach of ordinary people. In May 1826 lotteries were abolished by Parliament after 150 years.

The very **LAST LOTTERY BUT ONE** that can ever be offered in this Kingdom, will be all drawn on the 3d MAY next.

T. BISH,

4, *Cornhill, and 9, Charing Cross, London.*   CONTRACTOR.

SIX Prizes of £21,000!

And other Prizes, amounting to £337,760, all to be drawn
In One Day, 3d MAY.

SCHEME.

2......of......£20,600....	are £41,200	
2............ 20,500............	41,000	
2............ 20,300............	40,600	
2............ 1,140............	2,280	
2............ 700............	1,400	
2............ 500............	1,000	
4............ 400............	1,600	
10............ 206............	2,060	
20............ 53............	1,060	
60............ 26............	1,560	
NO BLANKS! as each of the above, and every other Number, will have £6, being..................	} 204,000	

Each £20,600 to have £400 more.
Each £20,500 to have £500 more.
Each £20,300 to have £700 more.
Every Number to have £6.

17,000 Numbers.   £337,760

Two Tickets of each Number.

BISH'S GREAT LUCK!

The tide of Success continues to flow uninterruptedly to BISH's Offices; every Drawing produces him the gratification of announcing that he and HIS AGENTS have sold a very large portion of all the Prizes.

In the Lottery just ended, BISH Shared and Sold

7,340	. . .	Class A . . .	£20,000!
10,004	. . .	Class B . . .	£20,000!

On the 6th of December last, BISH Shared and Sold

TWO	. . .	Prizes of . . .	£30,000!

On the 18th of October last, BISH Shared and Sold

THREE	. .	Prizes of . . .	£30,000!

Within Eleven Months, BISH Shared and Sold

FIVE	. .	Prizes of . . .	£30,000!
ELEVEN	. .	Prizes of . . .	£20,000!

TICKETS and SHARES are Selling by BISH, the Contractor, at his London Offices, No. 4, Cornhill, and No. 9, Charing Cross, and by his Agents,

J. GIBBS, Auctioneer	AYLESBURY.	Mrs. H. ELKENS, Stamp Office . .	READING.
H. SLATTER, Bookseller	OXFORD.	R. HEDGES, Auctioneer	THAME.

Almost weekly we read about the sale of furniture and effects. Often this was when someone had died, but also when people moved house; anyone moving to another town sold everything, which was probably cheaper than moving furniture long distances on poor roads. There were appeals for charitable causes and lists of local men and women who donated to them, including the sums they had given.

On the first page of the first issue Charles Knight Jr also published his statement of intent:

It will be the endeavour of the editors of the paper:
1. To collect and arrange such political facts and economical facts as from their nature are obscure and undigested, and yet are of essential importance to be understood.
2. To furnish a weekly summary of political events, with such remarks as may assist in forming a right judgment in objects of universal interest.
3. A faithful abridgement of the Parliamentary debates will be provided.
4. The domestic occurrences of the week will be carefully selected.
5. To report on the general agricultural and commercial price reports of the kingdom and the principal markets in surrounding counties.
6. The state of the public funds will be diligently collected and accurately reported.
7. Miscellaneous articles of general literature will at times be provided for the amusement of the subscribers.

Turning to page two we find international news, reports from Parliament and political opinions, which often spilled over to page three. There were dispatches from the war in the early years. The second issue for instance carries the news of the war with America and dispatches from Salamanca. News of the defeat of Napoleon at Waterloo covers pages two to four in the issue dated 18-25 June 1815.

There were often reports of petitions made to Parliament or the Monarch. Petitions on Catholic emancipation, which were frequently debated in both Houses, were presented with equal passion with pleas for and against.

Page three was dominated by news from around the country, various Assizes from the shires, or reports from the Old Bailey. There were also reviews of books, theatres or the latest opera, and often a column called 'miscellaneous' which carried tit-bits of odd news-items.

Page four contained local news, but given the wide distribution of the paper, two issues of this page were printed: one for Berkshire and one for Buckinghamshire. But local news was not given the predominance as today in local papers. There was, however, always a report on the Royal family. The early years were dominated by news about the condition of King George III who was languishing at Windsor Castle until his death in 1820. There were reports of Royal hunts and the occasional cricket match, rowing event or horse races, but sport did not feature greatly in the paper. It also contains commodity prices and announcements of births, marriages and deaths, and frequently a mixture of news left over from the other pages.

The Knights were careful to toe the line, never criticizing the government or rocking the establishment. There was no such thing as freedom of the press and publishers had been known to end up in gaol. One feature of the early issues was the *Political Inquirer*, printed most weeks on page two. This possibly more than anything else reflects the voice and opinions of Charles Knight Jr. He was always critical of dissent, but he would speak sympathetically in support of the underdog, for instance the weavers when they were in distress during the early 1820s. However when they advocated strike actions or made radical speeches, he **had** to be critical of them.

The town

What sort of town was the Windsor on which the Knights launched their newspaper in 1812? Clearly very different from the town we know today; even the Castle looked different then. It was in poor repair and tourists and locals alike were able to wander freely through it. The population was of course much smaller. The first census taken in England in 1801 gave the population of Windsor as 3,197, of Clewer 1,695 and the Castle as 239, a grand total of 5,131. About 25% of these were soldiers and their families. But by the time when Charles Knight Jr left for London in 1827 the population had increased to almost 8,500.

The older Charles Knight showed a great interest in the town and within five years of settling here in 1780 he produced the first *Windsor Guide*. The Castle had always been a tourist attraction and during the eighteenth century the new turnpike roads and improved coach travel brought more visitors to Windsor than ever before; Knight must have realized that a guide would be a good seller. In fact this book ran into many editions over the next 50 years. The early editions give us a glimpse of the appearance of Windsor before the railway came to the town and before the drastic changes made by George IV to Windsor Castle.

The *Windsor Guide* starts by saying:

Windsor is delightfully situated in the county of Berks, 22 miles west of London, on the verdant bank of the mild and gentle river Thames, which from its serpentine course in this part of it was, in King Edward the Confessor's charter, termed Windlesora, (the Winding shore).

11

This is a **Windsor** guide, and does not include Clewer, therefore Knight justly said that Windsor has only 6 streets:

> The town of Windsor consists of six principal streets, viz Park Street, High Street, Thames Street, Peascod Street, Church Street and Castle Street, all of them well disposed, paved and lighted in the same manner as London, by virtue of an Act of Parliament passed in 1769. The less considerable streets are Butcher Row (lately called Queen Street), St Albans Street (formerly named Priest Street), Sheet Street, George Street, Beer Lane (now called Red Lion Street) and Datchet Lane. These streets and lanes are but partially lighted and indifferently paved.

He described the old parish church as 'a spacious, ancient, ill-built fabric, with pews so constructed as to exclude a majority of the inhabitants from attending divine service.'

Windsor was a small market town dominated by tradesmen and craftsmen who served the Castle and the two barracks. Charles Knight Jr was less enamoured of Windsor and called it in his recollections *Passages of a Working Life* 'essentially a country town of the narrowest range of observation and the tiniest circle of knowledge'. He thought it was provincial. But it was also like other British towns, experiencing rapid growth and with it the growth of slums and increasing poverty.

He described the houses crowded in the castle ditch as 'of the meanest character and with the most disreputable occupiers'. George Street however, was the worst: 'There was a whole street of a vicious population where almost every house was a den of infamy. At the bottom of this foul quarter stood our gaol.'

Charles Knight Jr was aware of and very concerned about the plight of the poor. He recalled a bread riot in Windsor when he was a small boy:

> The misery of the poor at the beginning of the century was sufficiently visible even to my childish apprehension. ...I was returning home from a game in the Park, I heard the distant shouts of a multitude and saw a furious mob gathering in the market place.
>
> I got into the safety of my own home none too soon, for the mob was coming towards the baker's shop that was next door. They had smashed the windows of the bakers in the lower part of the town. They believed... that the high price of corn was wholly occasioned by combinations of corn- factors, meal-men, millers and bakers; and that if these oppressors of the nation could be compelled to bring their stores to market, there would be abundance and cheapness, and no possible chance of the supply falling short.

Poverty and slums were to dog Windsor throughout the nineteenth century. Two particularly bad years occurred during this period, 1812 and 1816, which was the year without a summer after the eruption of the volcano Tambora in April 1815, the largest in recorded history. On page two of the 19-20 November issue there is a small report from Batavia of the eruption of the volcano Mt Tomboro [sic]. The unusual weather in 1816 was under-reported in the newspaper, but the economic recession and the record number of bankruptcies which occurred during 1816 were; the demise of the Windsor bank of Brown & Coombs was covered in depth.

The Castle was in a poor state. The first two Georges had neglected Windsor, only visiting for the Garter ceremony. After 1760 when George III became king, Windsor again received royal favour; but the King and his large family who came regularly to the town found that the Castle was cold and draughty. Although it was made habitable, they moved into Queen Anne's House opposite the South Terrace, and renamed it Queen's Lodge. It had to be extended which gave it an appearance rather like a barrack block. Furthermore, Burford House, which had been built for Nell Gwynn was bought from the Duke of St Albans in 1779; this finally provided enough space for George's growing family.

Queen's Lodge was pulled down by George IV during his improvements to the Castle in the 1820s by James Wyatt. This was widely reported in the paper along with the controversy of the huge cost it incurred.

The newspaper carried regular features and the occasional reader's letter about the poor state of the town, and suggestions about improving matters. However, during the period nothing much was done, other than the castle improvements.

The publishers

The *Windsor and Eton Express* was founded by Charles Knight and his son in August 1812. Charles Knight Jr is better known as one of the most enterprising publishers and booksellers of the 19th century, a pioneer in popular literature, involved with the *Society for the Diffusion of Useful Knowledge*, publisher of the *Penny Magazine*, the *Penny Cyclopaedia* and *Library of Entertaining Knowledge,* etc. Much is known and has been written about his achievement in this field, but here we will only concentrate on his and his father's life and work in Windsor.

Between them they lived in Windsor a mere 47 years, from 1780 to 1827 when Charles Knight Jr left for London to take up the work he is most renowned for, that of publishing popular literature.

Charles Knight senior 1750 - 1824

The portrait of Charles Knight Senior which hangs in the Mayor's Parlour at the Windsor Guildhall

Reproduced by permission of Royal Borough of Windsor & Maidenhead Civic Collection

He was born around 1750. Little is known about his birth and early years. His son said he never spoke about his childhood. However, there is a rumour that he was born in Windsor and was the illegitimate son of Frederick Prince of Wales, eldest son of George II and one Henrietta Knight. However, there is no firm evidence to support this. What **is** known is that Prince Frederick had a liaison with a Miss Knight shortly before he died in 1751, and that Henrietta Knight, daughter of the honourable Henrietta St John Knight, had been friendly with the Prince.

Another factor that aids the credence of the rumour is that George III, eldest son of Frederick, gave the wealthy living of the rectory of Moor Monkton in Yorkshire to the Rev. James Hampton and Charles Knight was put into his care. The only problem is, that the Rev. Hampton left his church in charge of a curate and lived it up in Knightsbridge. So, if Charles Knight grew up in Yorkshire he would have been cared for by the curate. Did he have a Yorkshire accent? We don't know. But on the death of the Rev. Hampton in 1778, Charles inherited a considerable legacy, and with it he was able to set himself up in Windsor in the year 1780 as a bookseller and printer at 2 Castle Hill. It was here that George III paid him informal visits, perhaps as one brother to another, though unacknowledged.

And there is the portrait. This is quite an informal portrait of Charles Knight Sr as a young man, but why is he wearing the Windsor uniform?

In 1789 Knight married Mary Binfield and their son Charles was born in 1791; sadly Mary died just over year later in 1893. He never got over her loss and never re-married.

It may have been the death of his wife that made Knight look for something to do, for other responsibilities beside his publishing and bookselling. He was one of Windsor's leading businessmen and soon became a freeman of the town, thus on 12 October 1793 he was elected a member of the Windsor Corporation. Knight attended every Council meeting and steadily rose through the ranks: in 1797 he was elected Bailiff, in 1803 he became Bencher, Alderman in 1805 and Mayor in 1806.

His son remembered that much of his father's time was spent on public affairs, both of the parish and of the corporation. He was again elected Mayor in 1817. This means he was also the local Magistrate and in this capacity persuaded his son to be Overseer of the Poor.

Other senior positions he held were:

1808 and 1818 Justice of the Peace

1823 and 1824 Bailiff

In October 1824 he last signed the Hall Book (Council Minutes), one month before his death.

Charles Knight was also a lieutenant in the local volunteer corps during the Napoleonic Wars. His son remembered:

> I was ever at his side in those midsummer marchings. He had to pipe-clay his white breeches and gaiters. He had to polish the bright barrel of his musket till he could see his face in it like a modern footman; and then to wash the grease and flour out, till he was fit to stand at the counter or sit at the desk like an honest tradesman.

Then he marched all the way to 'Bulmarch Heath' near Reading to take his place amongst the other 'bold warriors of Berkshire'.

Before he ventured into publishing a newspaper he had tried publishing other journals. In 1785 he was involved in the *Microcosm* a paper written by Etonians, and edited by George Canning, later Prime Minister. During the 1790s he published *The Windsor Advertiser*, which carried a lonely-hearts section.

Seven years after first publishing the *Windsor and Eton Express,* in July 1819 he retired and handed over the newspaper to his son and Richard

15

Dredge. The paper carried a small announcement, which said that Charles Knight 'thanks his customers for their support in his stationery and newspaper business over 40 years'.

A year later, on 13 August and again 22 October 1820, Mr Tebbot the auctioneer advertised a large collection of books, paintings and prints etc, also a barrel organ for sale by Mr Knight on account of his 'declining business'. He died in November 1824 aged 74.

On the 27 November there was a simple announcement which read: 'died, on Monday last at his house in Sheet Street after an illness of 5 weeks, Charles Knight senior in his 74th year. He was twice mayor of Windsor and has lived in the town for 45 years'.

There is no obituary to him in the Windsor paper, nor in the *Reading Mercury* which also simply announced his death. Some months later, after Charles Knight Jr had sold the paper, the *Mercury* tried to buy the Windsor paper, declaring they had not done so before, out of respect for Charles Knight Sr.

Charles Knight Sr left no will but a number of unanswered questions.

Charles Knight junior [1791-1873]

*Watercolour portraits by John Collingham Moore of
Sally Vinney and Charles Knight Jr
Royal Borough of Windsor & Maidenhead Civic Collection*

These two portraits were bought by the Friends of the Windsor & Royal Borough Museum and are at present hanging in the Mayor's Parlour at the Windsor Guildhall.

Charles Knight Jr grew up in Windsor, raised by his father and a 'faithful servant'. Despite the early death of his mother, he spent a happy childhood roaming the Park, the Castle and Terrace, which was then open for anyone to wander around.

His father took him to meet the astronomer William Herschel, (who then lived at Slough) and to London and the theatre, which he loved all his life. In his father's bookshop, surrounded by books, he soon learned to read, and from an early age to love and value books. He became convinced that books were the key to social reform, which could only come through education; the answer, he believed, was to bring good literature within the reach of all at a price everyone could afford. This was to be his life's work.

At the age of 14, after schooling in Windsor and Ealing, he was apprenticed to his father. He learned not only the printing trade, but dealing in new and second-hand books and buying private libraries. In 1811, just 20 years old, he catalogued the library of the Countess of Orkney at Cliveden. Early in 1812 he spent a few weeks in London as a journalist for the *Globe* newspaper. The intention of starting their own newspaper must have already been discussed and planned by father and son, and it was perhaps with this in mind that the son was sent to London.

For the first few years Charles Knight Jr was the only reporter and wrote most of the features; articles were also copied from other newspapers around the country. He was not always treated with respect as a reporter. In November 1817 he was to report on the funeral of Princess Charlotte and had a pass for St George's Chapel, but he was 'haughtily repulsed'. 'collared like a felon' and 'thrust against a carriage like an intrusive hound', when he tried to get past the military who were guarding the entrance to the castle. He later claimed that most of the soldiers had been drunk.

Like his father Charles Knight Jr was very public-spirited. Though he did not get involved in the Council chamber, he cared deeply about local issues. He was particularly interested in anything to do with helping the less well off or promoting education. He was secretary of the Bible Society, treasurer of the Windsor Association for the Prosecution of Felons and Thieves, he promoted the National School, the Windsor Dispensary and a savings bank for the industrious working classes. Subscription lists with donations for good causes were published in the paper and his name was always among the donors.

During Charles Knight Sr's second term in office as Mayor, he persuaded his son to take the post of Overseer of the Poor, a job he did not relish, but which he agreed helped him to gain an insight into the lives and the condition of the poor of his town. He took it very seriously, visiting the 'out poor', something that apparently had not been done before.

He was also very enterprising. He used the bookshop not just to sell the books he advertised in the paper, but sold theatre tickets, acted as agent for fire insurances, sold patent medicines and much more. He also continued publishing his father's *Windsor Guide*; in April 1825 he advertised a new edition, price four shillings.

After his father retired at the age of 70, he went into partnership with Richard Dredge with whom he opened a reading room and circulating library, but the partnership only lasted four years.

On 13 April 1822 there was a disastrous fire in Sheet Street, which started in Knight's stables and spread to the adjoining eight tenements. It left 72 poor people homeless. He immediately set up a subscription list for them, but also thanked the soldiers from the nearby barracks who helped to put out the flames, saving part of his stables and coach house.

In 1825 he lost a libel action, after falsely reporting that a butcher and his wife had been convicted of a violent assault, when in fact they had been acquitted. Knight was fined £50. Ever the honest man, he reported the case in full in his paper.

In 1827 he finally gave up struggling with financial setbacks, fighting with bureaucracy and petty restrictions about what he could and could not print, and sold the paper to William Henry Reynell, who sold it to John Burris Brown and Richard Oxley in August 1833. The Oxley family published the paper until the 1980s.

Charles Knight Jr reveals little about himself in his autobiography *Passages of a Working Life,* neither does he use the newspaper to promote himself; he was a very private man. His marriage in 1814 is not announced in his newspaper, although there is a column for notices of births, marriages and deaths. Nor are his children's births or deaths mentioned in the paper, and he had seven children: five were born in Windsor and two died in Windsor and were buried in the family tomb.

After he sold all his possessions he moved to London. But he did come back, he is buried in Windsor, and the *Express* carried a lengthy obituary.

The Knight Family Tomb on Bachelors Acre
Express Photograph

The Newspaper Files

The newspapers are bound into volumes of two-year periods. The early ones have been restored through the initiative of the Windsor Local History Group with donations from the Royal Purse, Rotary groups, Royal Albert Institute to private individuals. The Charles Knight volumes, 1812-1829 are bound in red and boxed. Others are bound in plain grey. There are, however still some volumes that need attention.

Advertising

Advertising, much the same as today, provided the main income for the newspaper. Some of the papers in the archive have handwritten numbers which are probably customer numbers, and amounts of money which seem to give the price of adverts which would be invoiced later. Some say an amount of money and 'Paid'. These were probably from a customer who paid in cash before publication. One issue of 1822 was marked in this way and would have provided an income of over £27 if all the bills were paid.

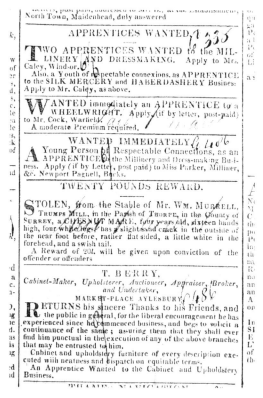

The front page was usually filled with advertisements and announcements and occasionally these spilled onto other pages. It was not until September 1939 that the front page was given over to news. These were what we would now call classifieds but they were mixed together with jobs, apprenticeships, articles for sale and meetings side by side. Most common were houses for sale or to let and the sale of house contents. On page one of the first issue we find that the Willows at Dedworth was offered 'to let for seven years', and four lots of household furniture and effects were for sale.

Not only on the death of a householder were furnishings and effects sold, but anyone who moved away sold all their possessions, as did Charles Knight when he moved to London. Charles Knight put his house up for sale with an advertisement in the newspaper in May 1827 as 'A truly valuable and elegant cottage residence' with four acres of land. It was in Sheet Street, backing onto the Great Park. The following week he advertised 'The excellent and appropriate Furniture, gig and harness, dung cart, and other effects'.

A year later the estate was still not sold, and offered again for sale at auction on 31 July 1828. One assumes the house finally found a buyer, but we do not know what happened to it. There is no trace of this house now.

Sales by Auction.

MODERN COTTAGE VILLA,
WITH LAND, IN THE IMMEDIATE ENVIRONS OF
THE TOWN OF WINDSOR,
ALSO AN ESTABLISHED SHOP.
With early Possession.

TO BE SOLD BY AUCTION,
Upon the Premises,
On THURSDAY, JULY 31st,
BY ORDER OF THE
TRUSTEES of the ESTATE of Mr. CHARLES KNIGHT,
(Unless an acceptable offer should be previously made
by private Contract.)

A DESIRABLE MODERN RESIDENCE, on a compact comfortable scale, with various out offices, stabling, coach-house, cattle buildings, LAWN, PRODUCTIVE GARDENS, and about FOUR ACRES of REMARKABLY RICH MEADOW and ORCHARD GROUND, luxuriantly stocked with the CHOICEST FRUIT TREES, presenting altogether an enviable little retreat, such as is scarcely to be obtained so near the town, pleasantly situated on one of the principal approaches to the Great Park, overlooking the celebrated Long Walk, commanding a magnificent view of the Castle, St. Leonard's-hill, &c.

Also, a DOUBLE DWELLING HOUSE and established SHOP, nearly in the centre of the town, in the occupation of Mr. Grantham, grocer, most advantageously situated for any kind of business.

For Particulars, &c. apply to
DANIEL SMITH and SON,
Land Agents, &c. Windsor and Alderman's Walk, London.

NOTICE OF AN EXTENSIVE SALE.

THE FIRST PART OF THE
VALUABLE MATERIALS,
AND
Capital Fixtures,
OF
AUGUSTA LODGE,
WITH ITS
SPACIOUS WINGS, STABLES, COACH-HOUSES, &c.
ST. ALBAN'S-STREET, WINDSOR.

*Which, by Order of the Surveyor-General of his Majesty's
Board of Works,*

Will be Sold by Auction,
By Mr. TEBBOTT,
On MONDAY, the 6th day of MAY, 1822,
And FOUR FOLLOWING DAYS,
Each Day at Twelve o'clock,
Without the least Reservation,—in Lots suitable to every
description of Purchasers,
To be taken down at their own Expense;

THIS NOBLE PILE OF BUILDING contains an immensity of choice internal *Finishings,* executed in a superior manner, and with materials of the first quality;—consisting of *One Hundred and Forty* Squares of seasoned clean Deal and Second Floors; *One Hundred and Forty* Sash-frames, glazed, with the best glass, with boxed shutters, &c.; *One Hundred and Thirty* Doors, with the best mortice, brass and iron-rim locks, together with the linings and architraves; *a superior* clean Deal Staircase, with Spanish mahogany rail; *Four* Secondary Staircases; *Ten* Water Closets, completed in the best manner, with mahogany seats, cisterns, &c.; *Sixty* Closet Fronts, with shelves, &c.; *some Thousand Feet* of Dado; Wainscoting, Boarding, Canvas, and neat Papering of the Rooms; *Fifty-six* Marble and Portland Chimney Pieces, with slabs and shelves; *Two Thousand Four Hundred Feet* of Portland and York Paving (the most part equal to new).

ALL THE CAPITAL FIXTURES;
Comprising about *Fifty* Register and other Stoves; Smoke-jacks; *Two* Kitchen Ranges; Ovens; Hot plate; Stewing-stoves; Copper Boilers; Stone Sink; Cisterns; and other valuable appendages.
The Fittings of a Four-stall Stable; and about *One Hundred Yards* of Dutch Clinker Paving.

When a property was demolished, every stick and stone was sold, with the buyer expected to carry his purchases away. The sale from Augusta Lodge, which had been home to Princess Augusts, in April 1822 included 140 sash frames, 130 doors and five staircases.

Many of the advertisements were Public Notices and many of them in 1814 were about the local Enclosure Acts. By the time the *Express* was first published the strip system of agriculture was on its last legs. The paths between the strips were valuable agricultural land and an increase in population meant that it was important to use it to grow food crops.

In many parts of the country these strips were enclosed in the seventeenth and eighteenth centuries. But the Act for this area was not passed until 1813. A Commissioner was appointed for each parish and they put notices in the newspaper with details of the meetings they held in public houses. Enclosure notices for Windsor, Clewer, Old Windsor, Winkfield, Sunninghill and Winnersh appeared in the *Express* in January 1814. They spelled the word Inclosure in those days.

> *New Windsor and Dedworth Inclosure.*
>
> JAMES FAUGOIN, Commissioner.
>
> NOTICE is hereby Given, that all Persons and Bodies Corporate respectively, who have any Claims to Common and other Rights in, upon, or over any Lands or Grounds situate and being within the Parish of NEW WINDSOR, and the HAMLET of DEDWORTH, in the County of Berks, which are intended to be divided, allotted, and inclosed, under and by virtue of an Act of Parliament, passed in the last Session for vesting in his Majesty certain parts of Windsor Forest in the County of Berks, and for inclosing the Open Commonable Lands in the said Forest, are hereby required to deliver to the said Commissioner, at his next Meeting, to be held on Tuesday the first day of March next, at Eleven o'Clock in the Forenoon, at the House of John Lillewhite, called the Swan Inn, in NEW WINDSOR aforesaid, an Account or Schedule in Writing, signed by them, or their respective Husbands, Guardians, Trustees, Committees or Agents, of such their respective Rights or Claims; in which must be described the Lands and Grounds, and the respective Messuages, Lands, Tenements and Hereditaments, in respect whereof they shall claim to be entitled to any, and which of such rights, in and upon the same, or any part thereof, with the Names of the Persons in the Possession thereof, and the computed quantities of such Lands, Grounds and Estates, the nature and extent of such right, and in what right and for what Estates and Interests they claim the same, distinguishing the Freehold from the Copyhold or Leasehold ; and in default thereof, all and every Person and Persons so neglecting, will be totally debarred and excluded, of and from all right and title, in or upon the Lands, so to be divided, allotted and inclosed; and all benefit and advantage in or to any Share or Allotment thereof.
>
> By order of the Commissioner,
>
> JOHN SECKER, Clerk.
>
> Windsor, January 10, 1814.

The Bachelors of Windsor organised a petition against a proposed enclosure of the Acre. (January 1814). The Bachelors won, but a small part of the Acre was clipped away to make room for the New Road, now Victoria Street.

Sales of agricultural products featured not just during harvest times. 'A rick of Clover Hay and Three Mines of very Capital Spit Dung' was for sale by auction 'in the Yard at the bottom of Goswell Lane'.

Charles Knight advertised his books and magazines in the *Express* even after he had sold the paper, and coach companies made regular appearances. There were four advertisements for fire insurance on the same page in March 1815.

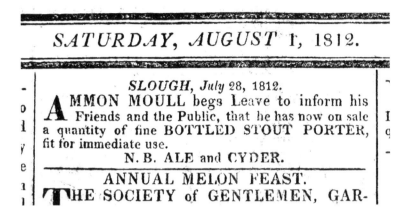

SATURDAY, AUGUST 1, 1812.

SLOUGH, July 28, 1812.

AMMON MOULL begs Leave to inform his Friends and the Public, that he has now on sale a quantity of fine BOTTLED STOUT PORTER, fit for immediate use.

N. B. ALE and CYDER.

ANNUAL MELON FEAST.

THE SOCIETY of GENTLEMEN, GAR-

Most of all, advertisements tell us about the commercial side of Windsor, the businesses large and small which advertised their wares or services in the newspaper. In the first issue Ammon Moull of Slough recommends his 'Bottled Stout Porter' to his customers, and J Warren, watch and clock maker of Castle Street was looking for an apprentice. In February 1817 J. Gunn, having established a coach factory in Brocas-Lane, Eton, humbly solicits the patronage of the Nobility, Gentry, Innkeepers and the Public in general: and pledges himself to execute any orders he may be favoured with, 'in a very superior style'. This wording was typical of many of the trade advertisements.

In March 1822 Alder, perfumer, hair cutter and ornamental hair manufacturer of 40 High Street recommended an assortments of shells, ivory combs and foreign perfumery.

Caleys had regular advertisements but they had many competitors, several of whom had Royal Warrants too. There was 'Linen Drapery and Silkmercery' W. Smith & Co at the bottom of Peascod Street, and J Keilor, tailor and draper in Thames Street, opposite George Street, who told his customers in March 1817 that he had 'a large assortment of new and used wearing apparel'. He also made clothes to order, from 'superfine coats' at £3 to pantaloons at 16s. Draper Samuel Harvey of Thames Street did not survive the slump of 1816, his household effects were offered for sale in March 1816 when he went bankrupt.

Wine and spirits were regularly advertised. The Castle Inn offered 450 dozen 'of very superior Old Port Wine' laid down for the late King in 1812, also 100 dozen claret, sherry and hock.

Tax on alcohol was reduced in 1825. The White Hart Inn announced a reduction of 1s 6d per bottle on wine following the budget. William Clode was selling port at 30s, claret at 42s and sauternes at 50s per dozen.

Wine even joined the long list of medications advertised in the paper; in April 1825, customers were assured that a new French Tonic and Digestive Wine 'affords relief in Indigestion, Scrofula, Worms, Nervous Debility and Head-aches', it even promised to 'prevent tipsiness and injurious effect of hard drinking'. Bottles 6s and 11s from R Calvert, tobacconist, 38 Thames-street. Could this have been a cordial?

But there were also the more unusual ones:

WANTS a Situation, as WET NURSE, a healthy YOUNG WOMAN, with a good Breast of Milk.

Letters directed (post-paid) for T. H. at Mr. NASH's, Blacksmith, Sunninghill, Berks, will be respectfully attended to.

18 September 1814

THE NORTH STAR, the property of Mr. W. SHERLEY, WILL COVER THIS SEASON, 1826, at Staines, Middlesex, at Two Sovereigns the Mare and Half-a-Crown the Groom. The NORTH STAR is a beautiful Bay Horse, rising four years old, 16 hands 2 inches high, of great substance and very superior action, and equal, if not superior, to any Horse of his years. His dam by Volunteer, was got by Victory.

15 April 1826

Illustrations

The number of illustrations in these newspapers was very small. Photography had not been invented and each illustration had to be hand carved on a wooden block. In the first issue the only picture was the Royal Arms on the masthead.

Gradually the advertisers began to supply blocks and proudly added the Royal Warrants and then their own signs or logos. The first to appear were the signs of the insurance companies, which were known to many people because there were plaques on many buildings to show which company was paid to insure the building and would therefore find the means to put out a fire. (PM)

Then other companies began to illustrate their own advertisements like these:

TALLY HO!
NEW AND ELEGANT LIGHT POST COACH,
ONLY FOUR INSIDES, TO LONDON,
IN TWO HOURS AND A HALF.

THREE PIGEONS,
PEASCOD-STREET, WINDSOR.
J. WELLS, LINEN-DRAPER, HABERDASHER,
HOSIER, LACEMAN, and GLOVER

ARTICLES FOR THE TOILET.

FOR THE GROWTH OF HAIR

Castle and Court

The Royal Family

Town and Crown

Just as the Castle dominated the landscape of the town, so the presence of royalty affected the running of the town. The *Windsor Express* paid particular attention to royal activities, for most of this period featuring on its back page a weekly account of the family's doings, which chronicled their goings-out and comings-in and even minor indispositions. It also reported all the balls, banquets, bell-ringings and illuminations with which the town marked royal anniversaries – and with George III's large family there were a great many of these. Even the wedding anniversary of the King and Queen was celebrated, the paper not noting the irony of their not having seen each other for years. Royal funerals were reported at length. The tone adopted by the paper in writing about royalty was always one of great respect: only in the crisis of 1820 over the trial of Queen Caroline for adultery did any scandal enter its pages. Nevertheless, supplemented by what we know now, through the newspaper's pages a picture emerges of royal family history.

George III

When the *Windsor Express* was launched the King was in very poor health. He was 74 years old, lame, half-blind, half-deaf, and following the death in 1810 of his beloved daughter Princess Amelia from a form of tuberculosis, he had had a relapse into his so-called 'madness' (really the metabolic disease porphyria, unknown to doctors then). He was confined with his attendants to a suite of rooms on the sunless north side of the Castle. There were frequent bulletins on the King's health. In the first edition, under the heading 'HIS MAJESTY'S HEALTH' it is stated that:

> Soon after the last Monthly Report, his Majesty had a severe accession of his disorder, which quickly subsided, and his Majesty has since continued as well as before that attack.

It was signed by his doctors, H[enry] Halford, M[atthew] Baillie, W[illiam] Heberden, and J[ohn] and R[obert] Willis. These brothers were the so-called 'mad' doctors from Lincolnshire, whose father Francis was credited with 'curing' the King when he had his first attack in 1788-79.

On 20 August it was said that:

For the last month there has been little variation in his Majesty's
health. He eats and sleeps well, and takes much regular exercise.

Even though the Prince of Wales had been appointed Prince Regent in
February 1811 it was hoped that the King would recover, but slowly it was
realised that this was not to be. It was a tragedy for a King who had been very
popular, especially in Windsor, his favourite residence, where the 'Squire of
Windsor' enjoyed hunting and running his three farms in the Great Park. But
now everything had to be sold off. On the front page of the 14 February
edition of 1813 an auction was announced for all the King's 'LIVE and DEAD
STOCK'. The live stock consisted of cattle and the King's flocks of sheep
including his 'celebrated flock of PURE MERINOS' while the dead stock was
waggons, dung carts, harrows and other farming implements. The King's
prized pack of harriers (hunting dogs) was also to be sold.

Nevertheless the King's 75th birthday on 4 June 1814 was celebrated
with a regatta at Eton (as it still is) and Queen Charlotte gave 'a splendid
dinner at Frogmore', but of course the King did not attend. In fact the Queen
now never saw her husband – she had a horror of his condition though she
insisted that all due respect was accorded him.

And so it went on, year after year, with monthly bulletins recording the
King's health, sometimes better sometimes worse. A typical one reads:

The King was rather less composed than usual last week, but has
since resumed his tranquillity. (November 1815).

His appetite was generally good, and music became his companion as he
could still play his flute and harpsichord. He grew a long grey beard and
refused to shave it. Neither births, marriages or deaths in his family were
known to him. Then in October 1819 the *Express* recorded that the King had
been on the throne for sixty years, 'longer than any King of either England or
Scotland'. He had acceded to the throne on 25 October 1760 and we should
not think that he had reached a Diamond Jubilee, but in those days
celebrations of anniversaries and birthdays always began as the party entered
into the year not at the end. But the King was not to see the completion of his
sixty years as monarch.

George III in old age by Joseph Lee
Supplied by Royal Collection Trust /
© HM Queen Elizabeth II 2012

The Prince Regent and the Royal Dukes.

The Regency, a temporary measure at first, was confirmed in 1812 and from then on George Prince of Wales was in effect the monarch. He and his estranged wife, Princess Caroline of Brunswick, had one child, the spirited Charlotte of Wales, sixteen in 1812, and second in line to the throne. She was given an establishment, Cranbourne Lodge near Windsor, to keep her away from her mother, which she resented. There were six other royal dukes whose appearances in Windsor were duly noted in the paper: Frederick Duke of York, William Duke of Clarence (later William IV), Ernest Duke of Cumberland, Edward Duke of Kent, Augustus Duke of Sussex and Adolphus Duke of Cambridge. Not one of these lusty men had then any (legitimate) children.

One of the Regent's first acts in the town, recorded in the second edition of the paper, was to reinstate the Sunday promenades which had been a popular feature of life in his father's time. On summer evenings on the South Terrace of the Castle, a band would play and the King, with his wife and daughters, would walk round the assembled company talking and joking with Windsor's citizens, many of whom he knew by name. Now the promenade was to be held again, though in the Long Walk. On the first occasion the band of the 29th Regiment 'entertained the brilliant company with the most favourite airs'. The Queen and Princesses arrived in carriages, with Princess Charlotte in a sporty two-seater called a phaeton. There was nearly a disaster when in order not to inconvenience those assembled in the Walk, she drove onto the grass where 'the inequality of the green' nearly overturned her. The band played *God Save the King* and the 'Royal family passed slowly by'. The Regent himself arrived later that month at Frogmore Lodge with the Duke of Clarence to celebrate his birthday, while in the town there was a ball at the Guildhall, the band of the 29th again providing music.

There was nothing the Regent liked more than to put on full military uniform, and shortly after his birthday he donned his Field Marshal's array to review the 23rd Light Dragoons on Hounslow Heath, accompanied by his brother Frederick. The Regent rode 'his bay charger', while the Duke of York, Commander-in-Chief of the army, was mounted on a grey. It was a pity that it was raining, but nevertheless the 'cavalry made a fine appearance', manoeuvring 'in columns, charging and retreating in squadrons, skirmishing and charging in divisions'. Then the troops advanced in line and saluted, 'which was returned by the royal Brothers with their usual urbanity' (20 August). There were more such reviews in later years, by which time the

Prince, proud of the achievement of the army at Waterloo, somehow seemed to believe that he been part of it too.

For all his faults and absurdities the Regent possessed great humanity. He disliked the death sentence and was pleased whenever he managed to get it commuted. He intervened in less serious cases too, in March 1815 issuing a royal pardon to Thomas Haydon, who had been sentenced to two years hard labour in 1814 for stealing beer from Messrs Jennings' cellars in Windsor. In another act of compassion the Prince commanded a pension of half a guinea a week to be paid to Phoebe Hassel, 104 years old, 'who now sells gingerbread in Brighton' (2 November 1817). Phoebe was that curious phenomenon, a woman soldier, who had fought in the British army at the Battle of Fontenoy and in the American War of Independence. Though she had been wounded her sex was not discovered until she was condemned to be stripped and flogged for some misdemeanour, whereupon she was dismissed and lost her pension rights. She sold gingerbread, she said, to keep herself from the work-house (and lived till 1821).

An Attack on the Regent

In January 1817, after opening the new session of Parliament, the Prince was attacked in his coach by a stone-throwing mob as he made his way home, while gravel was thrown at the Life Guards and their horses accompanying him. Luckily the glass of the coach was exceptionally thick, and it crazed but did not break.

The attack followed a protest demonstration in the cause of parliamentary reform. Britain had won the Battle of Waterloo in 1815, but in the years afterwards struggled to regain economic balance. There was great deprivation and consequent unrest. Many thought that the remedy was to make the parliamentary voting system more representative of the people. Earlier that day protesters had gathered and marched, military-style, to the House of Commons with petitions for reform. As reported in the *Express* these were long parchment scrolls, which they carried like muskets over their shoulders.

Inside the House of Lords the Regent delivered the government's speech from the throne. He began by saying how much he regretted being obliged to tell them that no alteration had taken place in the state of the King's 'lamented indisposition'. He passed on to foreign affairs, noting the success of the fleet in bringing about the 'liberation of all Christian captives' in Algeria. There was also reference to the state of the nation, with tacit

Queen Charlotte by John Hopkins
Supplied by Royal Collection Trust /
© HM Queen Elizabeth II 2012

admission of unrest. However, the Regent wound up by declaring that he was 'convinced of the loyalty and good sense of the great body of his Majesty's subjects' and relied on their support:

> in upholding a system of law and government … [which] is acknowledged by other nations, to be the most perfect that has ever fallen to the lot of any people (2 Feb 1817).

He may have reflected on the irony of that confidence on his journey home. Afterwards a thousand pounds reward was offered for successful prosecutions resulting from identifications of rioters; guards at public buildings were doubled. Two weeks later the *Express* reported the shock of Windsor's Corporation at the event, and an address was presented to the Regent deploring

> these scenes of outrage and disorder so lamentably disgraceful to British Subjects, and so utterly repugnant to human beings in a civilised State.

It was signed by the Mayor, who at that time was Charles Knight Sr. It would take till 1832, after the death of George IV, for the first Reform Bill to be presented to Parliament.

Queen Charlotte and the Princesses

While the King languished alone but unaware in his apartment, life was not easy for Queen Charlotte or his four remaining daughters, Princess Augusta (44 years old in 1812), Princess Elizabeth (42), Princess Mary (36) and Princess Sophia (35). These spinster princesses were rather unhappy, though naturally none of that unhappiness found its way into the newspaper. All of them yearned for independence but were still subject to the control of their mother whose temper had become uncertain. In their youth marriages were expected, but the King was reluctant to lose any of his daughters and suitors were not encouraged. Only the eldest Princess, Charlotte, had made a match (with the Prince of Würtemberg in 1797). Their lot improved when the Regent, whom they all adored, negotiated allowances for them in 1812, but this did not please the Queen who discouraged them from social pleasures out of 'respect' for the King's condition.

The Queen herself escaped when she could to her house at Frogmore, which with the help of her artistic daughter Princess Elizabeth she had made a pleasant retreat from the harsh associations of the Castle. All the princesses had apartments in the Castle, but Princess Elizabeth had taken a lease on a 'romantic cottage' at Old Windsor, where she could indulge her passion for farming, and give parties. One of her most spectacular was reported in September 1816, when she entertained the royal family and 'the neighbouring nobility and gentry' to a 'splendid fête'. The *Express* surpassed itself in admiration of the 'elegance' of the decorations. A ballroom was created from the tent of the Indian leader Tippoo Saib (taken following his defeat and death at Seringapatam in 1799). Inside it was

> elegantly decorated with artificial flowers, intermixed with instruments of husbandry, and lighted with variegated lamps. Three splendid chandeliers... were suspended from the roof. The floor was elegantly chalked... Brilliant mirrors were placed on the walls, surrounded by evergreens and fruits, with trained vines loaded with the finest fruit.

Dancing continued till midnight, 'to the delightful harmony of the band of the Royal Horse Guards'.

All the royal women did what they could to help the poor and needy, usually with donations of money, but Princess Elizabeth had in 1809 set up the imposingly-named Female School of Industry in Old Windsor, to teach girls from poor families skills for future life as domestic servants. In October 1812 the Queen and Princess Mary went with Princess Elizabeth to inspect the school. The *Express* commented that it was 'an establishment which, by the benevolence of her Royal Highness, has materially contributed to the happiness and morals of the neighbouring children'. Five years later the Queen went to inspect at the Princess's cottage an invention to prepare hemp and flax which she thought could ultimately 'afford much employment to the poor' (3 August 1817).

Long-term improvements did not, however, fill empty bellies: when in January 1814 heavy snow made life even harsher than usual, the Queen led a distribution of food essentials to between eight and nine hundred of the desperately poor. Twenty-three hundredweight of meat, 800 loaves and 100 bushels of potatoes were provided. A more sustainable plan was launched in the winter of 1816 when a fund was set up to subsidise the sale of bread and coals to the 'infirm and industrious poor' (the feckless poor need not apply). The King was inscribed for a donation of £150, the Queen gave £100 and the Princesses £25 each (December 1816).

Princess Augusta
After Sir William Beechy

Princess Elizabeth
By Sir William Beechy

Princess Charlotte of Wales
By Denis Brownell Murphy

Princess Sophia
By Sir William Beechy

All four pictures
Supplied by Royal Collection Trust / © HM Queen Elizabeth II 2012

There had been a diversion a few weeks earlier when 'the celebrated carriage' of Napoleon Bonaparte himself was brought to Frogmore and the royal women were able to converse with his coachman and be 'highly amused at the French style of driving'. But most of the references to their doings consisted of recording of outings or 'airings' in carriages (English style of driving presumably). Thus, for example, in February 1813 after an illness, Princess Charlotte 'was well enough on Monday to take an airing for about an hour and a half' though she had been 'prevented from repeating her airing on Tuesday, by being afflicted with a head-ache and cough'. Perhaps the Princess's headache was a way of avoiding what to a 17-year-old would have been a boring winter drive round the Park. Her aunts also found their lives tedious, though two of them did in the end make marriages.

On 22 July 1816 forty-year-old Princess Mary married her cousin, William Duke of Gloucester. The wedding in London was marked in Windsor with 'the usual demonstrations of joy in ringing of bells and illuminations', and the Queen gave every child at Charity and Sunday schools 'a plum cake and a glass of ale' to celebrate the occasion. This marriage did not take the Princess far as the Duke's home was at Bagshot Park. Princess Elizabeth's marriage however, took her completely away. Early in 1818 and to everybody's surprise including her own she received a proposal of marriage from Frederic Prince of Hesse-Homburg. They had never met. The Queen, who was far from well, was furious at the thought of losing the daughter on whom she relied and blamed her for the proposal, but she was ultimately brought round by the Regent. The Princess made arrangements for her charitable causes and the wedding – husband and wife both tubby, neither young – took place on 7 April in the drawing-room of the Queen's House (later Buckingham Palace). The bride wore a dress made from 'very elegant and rich silver tissue', trimmed with Brussels lace and fastened at the waist with a 'brilliant and beautiful diamond clasp'. On her head was a 'superb plume of ostrich feathers, with a most beautiful bandeau of diamonds'. She was given away by her uncle, the Duke of York.

At the wedding the energetic Princess Augusta (she took daily rides in the Park rather than coach airings) was described as wearing 'a superb train dress, with a beautiful striped lavender tissue border'. This Princess was never to be an official bride, but with a house in St Albans Street she had a long-standing but discreet relationship with General Sir Brett Spencer. She once wrote to the Regent asking for permission to marry him privately, though whether she did so is unknown.

The saddest case was that of Princess Sophia who, denied access to eligible men, had in her early twenties become besotted with one of her father's none-too-young equerries, Colonel Thomas Garth. She became pregnant and bore a child in 1800 (her father believed she was suffering from a dropsy which he was told was suddenly cured when she ate roast beef!) The boy, at first fostered, was later adopted by his father and given his name. Rumours abounded, but found no expression in the *Express* until March 1829 when an article headed 'The mysterious affair' was reprinted from a London newspaper. This tells how when Tommy Garth was five years old 'a respectable widow lady' living in Clewer was asked to take charge of the boy during the holidays. Various directions were given, including for the child to be brought to the Castle terrace one day at a particular hour where someone unnamed took up the child and carried him into the Castle, later returning him. Nobody was identified but it was made clear that royalty was involved. It was hard on Princess Sophia to be aware of rumour and to know that no marriage would ever be possible for her. She was the frailest of the sisters, often confined to her home at Lower Lodge in St Albans Street by illness: only the previous month the paper reported that 'a severe calamity' had befallen her as she had lost the sight of one of her eyes.

Marriages, Births and Deaths

There had been an important marriage in 1817: that of Princess Charlotte of Wales, second in line to the throne, to Prince Leopold of Belgium. The Princess was an attractive but strong-willed young woman, whom her father struggled to control (and he was jealous of her popularity). He wanted to separate her completely from her mother: this was unjust, but Princess Caroline was a devious woman who once, infamously, had locked her sixteen-year-old daughter in a bedroom with an army officer and told the pair to amuse themselves. The solution for the Regent was to get her married. When negotiations with the Prince of Orange failed an alliance was agreed with Prince Leopold of Saxe-Coburg. As with royal weddings today there was excitement at the news: in Windsor a celebratory dinner was announced, to be held in the Town Hall on 8 April, with tickets at 7/6, diners to sit down at 4pm – meals were served earlier then.

The wedding took place on 2 May 1816 in a room in the Queen's House. A temporary altar was set up with candlesticks and gold plate brought from the Chapel Royal at St James's. The Prince Regent gave the bride away and the Archbishop of Canterbury conducted the ceremony. *Express* readers were told that the princess had worn a dress composed of 'magnificent silver lama on net, over a rich silver tissue slip, with a superb border of silver lama, the embroidery at the bottom forming shells and bouquets'. Her head-dress consisted of a wreath of rose buds and leaves 'composed of brilliants'. The couple thereafter lived at Claremont at Esher in Surrey and were very happy; within a year the princess had become pregnant and was on good terms with her father (helped by Princess Caroline having taken her departure for Germany).

Following the wedding the Queen's health declined dramatically and she was advised to go to Bath to take the waters; she went accompanied by Princess Elizabeth. This very time was, however, when Princess Charlotte's baby was due and the Queen worried about her as she looked very big. She was right to worry: on 3 November 1817 the princess went into a labour which lasted 50 hours and ended with the birth of a still-born son. The news went swiftly to the Regent, who was relieved to know that the princess herself was well. But five hours later she complained of great pain, and nothing could be done to save her. Her father was speechless with grief, but reported as insisting on seeing his daughter's body. The shock was so great however, 'as to excite great apprehension and alarm' about him.

There was an outpouring of grief throughout the country. The *Express* printed a lengthy *Monody* by an ST, which gave expression to the sudden destruction of youth and hope for the future. The poet says

> I mus'd not on the fall of earthly state,
> How brief, how vain, the race of pride and power;
> I thought alone of that appalling hour
> When princely youth and beauty bow'd to fate.

The funeral of the Princess and her baby son took place in St George's Chapel, following a solemn procession from Claremont, the roads lined with weeping onlookers. The coffin, when brought to the Chapel, was covered with red velvet and a black pall, and was born by eight Yeomen of the Guard under a canopy of black velvet. The Regent was too distressed to attend, so the principal mourners were Prince Leopold and the Dukes of York and Clarence. Women did not then take part in funerals, so the Queen and her daughters had the distress of hearing the sounds from the Castle, but not participating.

A meeting of Windsor's citizens agreed to send letters of condolence to the Regent, Prince Leopold and the Queen; the personal annoyance felt with the conduct of the funeral by the editor of the *Express* is described later.

Everyone was aware that this wasn't just a personal tragedy but a constitutional one too. There was now no second-generation heir to the throne, only a series of middle-aged Dukes, none of the married ones with any children. But three of the royal brothers, the Dukes of Clarence, Kent and Cambridge were unmarried, so hastily all acquired wives. Two of them, Kent and Cambridge, were wed on the same day in June, Kent to the sister of Prince Leopold, the widowed Princess Victoria of Saxe-Cobourg, and Cambridge to another German princess, Augusta of Hesse-Cassel. The ceremony was held at Kew Palace because the Queen was confined there in ill-health.

William Duke of Clarence, third in line to the throne, had had ten children with his mistress the actress Dora Jordan, but he had cast her off in 1811. He now made a marriage with Adelaide Princess of Saxe-Cobourg-Meiningen and the wedding took place on 11 July 1818. A daughter, Elizabeth, was born prematurely the next year but only lived briefly, and none of the Duchess's subsequent pregnancies succeeded.

By this date Queen Charlotte was seriously ill. She was suffering from dropsy and daily bulletins were being issued. She longed to return to Windsor from Kew, feeling that she should be near the King, but though efforts were made to adapt some carriage for the journey, nothing proved possible. In September the *Express* regretted that the Queen had taken up her residence at Kew in the first place, since now the Palace was enveloped in the unhealthy 'autumn exhalations of the river'. Her condition continued to worsen; she could no longer lie down comfortably and had to sit upright on a chair to breathe. Then on 17 November the Regent was summoned and the Queen died just after one o'clock in the afternoon holding the hand of her favourite son.

The issue of the *Express* which covered the funeral is one of the few that are missing, but the previous week the black-bordered paper detailed what preparations had been made. The Queen's body, wrapped in white satin, had been placed while at Kew in a coffin, which was then filled up with spices. Then it was taken to Windsor for the funeral on 2 December in St George's Chapel, the Royal Standard flying at half-mast and with black streamers. A long covered way was erected leading to a portico outside the Chapel, both lined inside and out with black. The Duke of York was to be chief mourner, the Regent again unable to attend because the stress had caused him to become seriously ill himself.

Afterwards the Queen's will was published: she had left Frogmore to Princess Augusta, and Lower Lodge in St Albans Street to Princess Sophia. Her jewellery was to be divided equally between the four daughters. Subsequently, while hunting for these jewels some of the King's regalia, his sword and Garter star, which had been missing, were discovered in a lumber room of the Castle (13 January 1819). The King, of course, locked in his mental disorder, was totally unaware of his wife's death.

In 1819 the earlier royal weddings bore fruit: Victoria was born to the Duke and Duchess of Kent, while the Duchess of Cambridge gave birth to a boy, George. Then in January 1820, while staying in Sidmouth in Devon, the *Express* reported that the Duke of Kent came back from a walk with 'boots soaked through with the wet' and did not change them, 'being attracted by the smiles of his infant Princess' with whom he engaged 'in fond parental play'. Whether from that cause or not he developed a chill and in a few days died from an 'inflammation of the lungs, so violent as to baffle the utmost efforts of medical skill' (30 January 1820). This was bad news enough, but more was to follow.

The Death of George III

Year after year the King's condition had changed little, though he was now virtually blind. But he could still play his musical instruments, sometimes dressed in black apparently in mourning for himself. Then early in 1820 his condition deteriorated, and the Duke of York wrote in alarm to alert his brother the Regent. Noting the Duke's arrival the *Express* drew the obvious conclusion: 'It is with the deepest regret that we state our apprehension ... that His Majesty is again seriously ill' (23 January 1820).

The Duke was with the King when he died on 29 January, a day still seen as significant as the anniversary of Charles I's execution.

Though he had been missing from the public scene for so many years there was a sense of shock at the parting from life of this much-respected father of his people. Shops were shut and people of high and low degree wore tokens of mourning. The black mourning bands on the *Express* almost doubled their width.

'The King is dead – long live the King!' But the news affected George IV so badly that for a day or two it was thought the new King might be Frederick I. The proclamation of the accession of George IV was made by the Mayor, George Davis, according to tradition from the Market Cross (where Victoria's statue is now), the Castle gates and the bridge, but with the King's body lying within the Castle there were no trumpeters. At a meeting called of the Corporation the Mayor said that 'the most silent tribute of affection to the present Monarch would be the most respectful'. He was so affected that he had to be led from the chamber.

Arrangements for the funeral followed swiftly after those of the Duke of Kent. The covered way to the Chapel was recreated, and a platform draped in black built, on which the coffin was conveyed for interment in the royal vault. Black draperies were everywhere. The evening of the funeral was misty, but the stars shone brightly when in an atmosphere of 'solemn gloom' the procession made its way by torchlight to the sound of gunfire, a flourish of trumpets and a muffled roll of drums. A detachment of the Royal Horse Guards, George III's favourite regiment, accompanied the coffin. No fewer than 30,000 mourners came to Windsor to pay their respects to the dead monarch.

Trial and Coronation

England had a new King to be crowned – but would there also be a crowned Queen? The King certainly had no intention of letting that happen and wanted to divorce her. After the Princess left for the continent reports came in of outrageous and immodest behaviour, and the government agreed to send emissaries out to look into the situation. Known as the Milan Commission they reported back that the rumours appeared to be true. The Princess had taken a lover, Bartolommeo Pergami, and had been living with him in a villa on Lake Como. But before anyone could act on this information the situation was complicated by the death of George III. The 52-year-old princess was now Queen Caroline.

Efforts were made to persuade her not to come to England: her supporter, Henry Brougham, leader of the Whigs in Parliament, was authorised to offer her an annual payment of £50,000 to stay away. But the Queen was determined to assert her rights, and egged on by the radical Mayor of London, Alderman Wood, she reached Dover on 5 June 1820 to a tumultuous welcome. Cheering crowds followed her everywhere she went: she was the darling of the anti-monarch, anti-government reformists. For the rest of 1820 the *Express* was dominated by news of the royal scandal but first expressed regret 'that the nation is thus suddenly plunged into the most violent ferment of opinion' (11 June 1820).

A bill was introduced to the House of Lords on 17 August to determine the Queen's guilt or innocence – guilt would result in divorce. She published an open letter to the King printed in full in the *Express*, protesting at the 'unparalleled and unprovoked persecution' she had been subjected to for many years (20 August 1820). Crowds of supporters cheered her arrival at the Lords, wearing black with a heavy white veil. Henry Brougham represented her, a lawyer whose opening speech in her defence was admitted even by enemies to be brilliant. Brougham was aware of her guilt, but this was an opportunity to attack, perhaps bring down, the Tory government. The first witness, Majocchi, an Italian who had been in her service, presented damning evidence for the prosecution, but cross-examined by Brougham he fell apart, constantly repeating 'Non mi ricordo' [I don't remember]. The whole of this testimony and cross-examination can be read in a special supplement brought out by the *Express*. One result of the fiasco is that other Italian witnesses waiting at Calais turned back when they heard about it.

As the trial proceeded support for the Queen grew throughout the country, especially in the disenfranchised towns of the Midlands and North. There were marches and demonstrations in her favour and loyal addresses sent her, even one from the 'Female Inhabitants of Bray' for which she sent grateful thanks. The unpopular King, mocked and scorned, retreated to Royal Lodge to avoid unpleasantness. Eventually a vote was taken on 6 November, and the Bill of Pains and Privileges as it was titled was passed but only by a majority of nine, many peers voting tactically in fear of an uprising if the Queen were found guilty. It was then clear to the government that the Bill must be abandoned: it would never pass the Commons where the King's own dirty linen would be sure to be put on display.

Three days of bell-ringing, fireworks and bonfires followed, with 'Majocchi' burnt as a guy. Slough, Datchet and Langley were all illuminated. But after a public meeting called by the Mayor, John Banister, Windsor sent its own address to the King 'expressive of the loyal and constitutional Fidelity to the Throne' (3 December 1820).

And then it was all over and the wild enthusiasm for the Queen faded. She had only ever been a figure-head for the radical cause. The King could now plan for his coronation and, never a modest spender, the *Express* reported that the cost of his robes would exceed £20,000, including payment for the 26,000 Astrakhan lambs' feet needed for black spots inside the furred robes (February 1821). Coronation Day, 19 July 1821, was an occasion of great splendour, the magnificently-arrayed King entering the Abbey under a canopy of gold to the singing of the Psalm 122. Windsor celebrated with a procession and an ox-roast, the meat distributed with beer and bread, and with 2,000 coronation cakes.

The Queen had been informed that she would not be crowned or even admitted to Westminster Hall. But to go she was determined, and on Coronation day set off in her coach with a few cries of 'The Queen, the Queen for ever'. But she did not have a ticket of admittance and was turned away by a determined door-keeper, facing some hissing and booing on her humiliating return journey. Her spirit was broken and almost immediately she became desperately ill. She died of an intestinal blockage on 8 August. The *Express's* editors must have debated the propriety of black mourning bands to the paper, compromising by using them only on pages 2 and 3 with the account of the death. There was concern as to where the Queen would be buried, and relief that she had asked for her body to be returned to Brunswick for interment. However there was 'tumult' in Knightsbridge, with Alderman Wood attempting to fasten a silver plate on the coffin lid engraved with the words CAROLINE OF BRUNSWICK : THE INJURED QUEEN OF ENGLAND.

King George IV heard the news of the death while on his yacht, the *Royal George*, waiting to cross to Ireland for what was to prove a triumphant visit. With some reluctance he agreed to wear a mourning band on his arm.

King George IV

Following the success of his state visit to Ireland the King went to Hanover, and then to Scotland where he was also warmly greeted. When he landed, wearing naval uniform, he sported a large thistle, with a sprig of heather in his hat. Sir Walter Scott welcomed him to Edinburgh with verses which the newspaper printed (10 August 1822). If not great poetry it expressed enthusiasm:

> Auld England held him Lang and Fast;
> And Ireland had a joyfu' cast;
> But Scotland's turn is come at last –
> Carle, now the King's come! [*carle*: cheer?]

Sir Walter was impressed with the King; in turn he would visit him at Royal Lodge and be shown the building works at the Castle, which the *Express* had no doubt 'must have proved to his taste and antiquarian knowledge' (21 October 1826).

The King did not travel far again, becoming something of a recluse at Royal Lodge, preoccupied with his building works and his relationship with his last mistress, Lady Conyngham. He did not like to be seen in public, conscious of his increasing bulk and unsteady gait, caused by gout-swollen feet and legs. But Windsor continued to celebrate his every birthday and anniversary with dinners and balls.

The rebuilding at Windsor Castle, at vast expense, is described separately, but George IV left his mark on the town in other ways. In 1823 a letter from Sir Thomas Lawrence was printed on the front page, in which the artist promised the greatest attention to his portrait of the King in his Garter robes (15 February) which was to be presented to the Corporation. This 'superb' portrait was installed in the Guildhall and could be seen, illuminated with 'additional brilliance', at a ball the next month (8 March 1823). It hangs there today, the largest and arguably the most accomplished of all the royal portraits. Later that year the paper referred to the plan by the King to create a statue on the top of Snow Hill 'in veneration for the memory of his revered father'. Richard Westmacott (later knighted) was to be the sculptor: the *Express* hoped 'that the costume will be that of an *English* King, and not of a Grecian non-descript' (22 November 1823). The foundation stone was eventually laid in August 1829, but the King never saw the great 'Copper Horse' (George III as a Roman emperor), as it was not finished until 1831.

In the last years of his reign the King enjoyed making 'picturesque improvements' to Virginia Water, including an 'elegant fishing-house' (22 April 1826). In June that year it was reported that he visited Virginia Water almost daily to enjoy the fishing. Safe from observers, he took his dinner in a 'newly-built and capacious boat' (24 June). At the end of 1827 he had new plans, to erect a Temple there, 'from a pure and chaste design made by himself' (8 December).

He continued his philanthropy, pardoning wrong-doers when possible. In 1823 he issued a pardon to Will Mason and Philip Watkins, who had been sentenced to death for forging a £5 note: instead they were transported to New South Wales. He gave generously to charities. In both April and July 1826, following an announcement that foreign silks could now be imported cheaply, he donated £1000 to the distressed silk workers of Spitalfields. He later decreed that all materials for Windsor Castle were to be of British manufacture: 100 yards of crimson velvet and 500 yards of green were commissioned (21 September 1827) with an order for silks of 'little less than £80,000'. Other causes claimed his purse: in April 1826 he had also given £1000 to cotton weavers in both Macclesfield and Blackburn, who had lost work through machine-breakers. In May a very different gift of £210 was sent to the Literary Fund Society for the 'relief of poor authors'.

In 1827 the King suffered great grief when his favourite brother and heir, Frederick Duke of York, died. There were more black borders in the paper and another internment in the family vault in St George's Chapel on a freezing January day. Against the advice of his doctors this time the King insisted on attending. His own health was now precarious with frequent attacks of gout (not helped by the quantities of cherry brandy which he drank, but in the days before invasive journalism the paper knew nothing of that). A cataract was removed from one of his eyes (19 September 1829) which may have helped him to continue to enjoy fishing at Virginia Water and visiting the animals of his menagerie (see later article). But in the early part of 1830 he became increasingly bed-ridden and dropsical, unable to lie down because of difficulty in breathing. He died on 26 June at the age of 67.

The *Express* assumed its mourning black edges, and wrote at length about the King's life and then his funeral. It began at 8.30 pm on 15 July with a procession making its way to the Chapel to the blowing of trumpets and solemn beating of drums. The coffin was flanked by guardsmen with flaming torches, the pall held by six dukes and four eldest sons of dukes. The Duke of Wellington carried the Sword of State. The new King, William IV, formerly Duke of Clarence, was chief mourner in a 'magnificent purple velvet cloak'. But the service was lengthy and after two hours, during the singing of an anthem, the King took his departure, signalling the firing of a rocket and minute guns echoing from the Long Walk. In his absence the coffin of King George IV was slowly lowered into the royal vault to join those of his father, mother, daughter, still-born grandson, four brothers and a sister.

Outside 'patrols of military' thronged the Datchet road all night, while 'vehicles of all descriptions' tried to make their way out of town.

In the darkness and confusion two opportunists, Charles Dyke a shoemaker, and John Seward a journeyman, managed to make off with, respectively, twenty and thirty yards of black cloth stripped from the funeral platform in the Lower Ward. But their large parcels attracted suspicion and they were arrested. Brought before the magistrates in the Guildhall the men gave as their defence that they believed the cloth was 'the property of anyone' after the funeral. After consultation it was admitted that there had been some 'unseemly scrambling' on an earlier occasion for possession of such cloth, so the magistrate discharged the men, but warning them against future misdemeanours. The black cloth was then returned to the 'proper authorities', who would no doubt have need of it again (24 July 1830).(HD)

Queen's Lodge

Queen's Lodge - in later years known as Upper Lodge - stood close to the Southern Terrace of Windsor Castle on the alignment of the Long Walk. Originally, the Long Walk did not lead straight to the Castle and the gates in front of the Lodge opened straight into Windsor Great Park.

This building started life as small mid-17th century house, which became Queen Anne's Windsor residence. Several alterations were made to the original building in the early 1770s but, in 1775, it was totally demolished and rebuilt for George III.

The new building was designed by Sir William Chambers, although George III may also have had a hand in part of the design. It was very barrack-like in its construction, with a very plain range to the east, and was entered through a north-facing Gothic-style porch. The Lodge consisted of 100 rooms and was occupied by King George III and his family between 1778 and 1808, it was demolished by George IV in August 1823 to extend the Long Walk.

The *Windsor Express* of September 1823 carried an advertisement for an auction for the sale of the building material from Queen's Lodge by order of the 'Surveyor General of His Majesty's Board of Works' which was to take place on 15 September. The sale was described as 'a most desirable opportunity of purchase to builders throughout the country'. It was possible to view the premises up to four days before the sale. Catalogues were sold throughout Berkshire, Buckinghamshire, Oxfordshire, Surrey and Sussex. They could also be purchased locally from Mr Tebbott's premises in Sheet Street, Windsor.

The most unusual part of the sale was that the auction took place within the standing building before it was demolished. The auctioneer was local builder Robert Tebbott who sold off different parts of the building in lots. The building material on offer '...was of the best quality suitable for first rate houses' and included:

'three hundred rods of brickwork; four thousand feet cube of Portland [stone] in Plinths, string courses, coping etc., several thousand feet of Portland and York paving and steps. One hundred marble and Portland chimney pieces, a spacious Portland staircase, with ornamental balustrade and mahogany rail...an elegant Portland Gothic porch... Three hundred circular and square headed sash frames and wainscot sashes, with shutters etc., about twenty thousand feet of wainscoting, dado and rough boarding, and thirty tons of lead. One hundred and sixty feet of capital iron palisade railing with stone plinths...'

Once the purchaser had bid for the lots he wanted it was his responsibility to take down his purchased materials.

After the building had been demolished George IV extended the Long Walk right up to the Castle's entrance. Nothing now remains of this former Royal Palace. (EK)

The Rebuilding of Windsor Castle

By the first quarter of the nineteenth century Windsor Castle was in a dilapidated state. It had not been occupied by the Royal family for over a hundred years. The last monarch to have carried out building work or repairs at the Castle was Charles II in the 1670s. Queen Anne had preferred a cottage known as the Garden House just outside the Castle walls, which was later, enlarged and occupied by George III and his family. It was then known as Queen's or Upper Lodge. The Castle and its terraces were open for the public to visit as recorded in Charles Knight's *Windsor Guide* of 1811.

In August 1819 the *Express* reported that one of the towers previously occupied by Princess Augusta had been taken down due to its decayed state. A large crack or 'chasm' as it was described in the paper had been discovered on the lower part of the outside wall. It was promised that 'The tower will be rebuilt upon the same plan'.

The *Express* of August 1823 reported that repairs and 'alterations throughout the palace had been very considerable' in readiness for George IV to take up residency at the Castle. These alterations included refurbishing the King's private apartments, music room, dining room and building a new kitchen. The terrace at Windsor Castle was going to close to the public to allow for preparations for the King's occupancy. Whilst the preparations were taking place he was in residence at Cumberland Lodge.

When the King moved into the Castle In October 1823, the event was celebrated by the illumination of shops, and ringing of the church bells. An ox roast for the poor was held on Bachelors' Acre. The King stayed in Windsor until November and celebrated 'Divine service in his private chapel in the Castle'. In December and January he stayed at Frogmore and at the Brighton Pavilion, returning to Windsor in February 1824. It was believed that he 'would continue to live at the Castle for a considerable time'. Indeed he did, for he was making plans for a major makeover of Windsor Castle.

the plans for these alterations are on an impressive scale. The architects of the Board of Works, and other distinguished artists, are preparing a series of drawings for the improvement of this majestic edifice.

In May 1824 Commissioners for directing the alterations were appointed and included the Duke of Wellington, and the Earl of Liverpool. After the Commissioners and the King had reviewed plans for the alterations, the designs drawn up by Mr Jeffry Wyatt were adopted in June 1825. They were chosen for 'the most careful attention to the proper splendour and comfort of its august possessor'. Two scale models based on Wyatt's plans were built by Robert Tebbott for the King; one showing the Castle as it was and the other showing the proposed improvements.

The new improvements started in earnest but it was soon found that the Castle needed major repairs. The *Express* reports that by early August 1824:

> the progress in dismantling the Castle during the last fortnight has been very rapid. The whole interior of the east and west sides with the exception of the staircases and a great part of the passages has been removed. The walls have generally been cleared of their wainscoting –

and they probably now remain in the state which they were previous to the repairs of the Castle by Charles II.

The removal of the panelling from an apartment between the York and Augusta Towers uncovered some very old frescoes including one depicting Queen Cleopatra. This was to be the first of many interesting discoveries unearthed during the reconstruction of the Castle.
On 14 August 1824, the King laid the first stone to the new entrance tower in celebration of his birthday. The *Express* describes the ceremony:

Upon the arrival of the Royal party at the Castle His Majesty was received by Mr Wyatt, the architect, and other principal persons employed in the projected improvements, the workmen forming a line round the spot. The block being prepared for fixing, Mr Wyatt presented the silver trowel, with which his Majesty having spread the mortar, a stone bearing the following inscription was lowered into its bed:

GEORGE THE FOURTH
BY THE Grace of God, King of Great Britain and Defender
Of the Faith,
Laid this Corner Stone of a new entrance to his Castle at Windsor,
Which has been for upwards of seven centuries
The residence of his Predecessors,
On the Sixty-second anniversary of his Birth-day,
August 12 1824
JEFFRY WYATTVILE, architect. '

The stone was then set in place and the King ordered that half-a-crown to be given to each of the workmen. During the early stages of demolition and lowering of the Castle-yard a hole was discovered which went down some twenty feet and a large (previously unknown) passageway was discovered which went under the Castle and its terrace. The King gave instructions for it to be cleared out. While digging in the south-eastern corner of the Upper Court a gold ring dating from the reign of Elizabeth I was found.

Invariably accidents happen during Castle restoration works. A carpenter by the name of Sargeant who was working near the top of the North East tower slipped from the scaffolding and fell some forty feet but only broke a leg (September 1824). On one day in September 1826 a glazier fell off a plank and broke several ribs and a man called Vickers was blinded for life by some mortar which 'burst in his face'. George Smith lost both his legs in an accident moving heavy stones at the Castle in January 1827.

Over the next few years there were frequent visits to inspect the alterations to the Castle by the Royal family as well as the Duke of Wellington. The paper reported in January 1825 that despite the inclement weather 'it gives us great pleasure to observe that the erections at the Castle are proceeding with extraordinary activity'. Works included the building of a new tower and gateway, known as the George IV Gateway leading from the Long Walk. Some of the Castle's buildings were heightened, notably the Round Tower, which was given an additional forty feet. *The Express* said that 'it is even now apparent that the additional height of the whole of the edifice will give it a character of magnificence, suited to its dignity as the most ancient palace of the British Kings'. Windsorians who had lived or worked in the shadow of the Castle must have been truly amazed by the new height of the tower which now acted as a major landmark that could be seen from a great distance away.

To keep building on track a large workforce of craftsmen as well as labourers were employed, some of whom were unscrupulous. The theft of raw building materials, especially lead, was regularly reported. In January 1826 James Manley was put on trial at the Quarter Sessions held at Windsor Guildhall for receiving 25lbs of lead, reputedly stolen, from the top of St George's Hall. As there was not enough evidence Manley was found 'Not Guilty'. In February 1828 some expensive plate glass from the visitor's entrance was stolen.

The rebuilding of Windsor Castle was financed from public funds. The King however, paid some money towards furnishing the Castle's interior. In March 1826 a motion was proposed in the House of Commons that £70,000 should be spent on the repairs. It was obvious that this was only a projected figure as the Chancellor reported that the total costs could not be predicted in advance. The expenditure for work at the Castle was not without its critics. During the debate William Hume 'could not help protesting against this sort of expenditure'. Windsor Castle should be allowed to remain as it was; 'its antiquity rendered it venerable'. Despite objections the Commons voted that a further £100,000 should be spent on 'those splendid works now in progress at Windsor Castle' (May 1827).

By the autumn of 1827 work had started on the interior decorative scheme for the newly refurbished state apartments. The King gave 'orders for silk drapery of British manufacture' to hang in the state apartments of Windsor Castle 'of the richest and most elegant description', the cost of which was said to be almost £80,000 (September 1827). The principal colour used was crimson velvet with tulip patterns. Parts of the apartments were decorated in green velvet with a similar tulip pattern.

In February 1828 the refurbishment was almost complete. A new entrance to the state apartments featured an ornate projecting canopy which led to a sweeping stone staircase, at the top were two large doors fitted with plate glass and wainscoting. This in turn led to an octagonal music room with tiered seating for a large band. Also completed were a large dining room and library, lit by large panes of glass inserted into gothic windows. The rooms were decorated by ornate mirrors placed opposite each other to give a feeling of grandeur and space. The side tables in the dining room were of rosewood, richly carved and inlaid with gold. Matching rosewood chairs had been brought down from Carlton House in London. The upholstery to these chairs matched the wall hangings in this room, which had been woven by Spitalfields weavers. Carpets of British manufacture were laid in the principal state apartments.

Work in progress in the state apartments included a new ballroom known as St George's Hall, which was described as being of lofty proportions 'inferior only in magnitude of its dimensions to Westminster Hall'. Also still under construction was the 'Waterloo Gallery' which was to house the King's art collection. It is interesting to note that whilst the work was taking place the King held his Court at the Castle in April 1828.

While the refurbishment of the state apartments was carried out, work was done landscaping and adorning the area around the Castle. This included a new semi-circular north-east terrace, flower gardens of two acres immediately in front of the state apartments, a gothic orangery with views across the garden and a new south wing to the state apartments. The centre of this wing fronted onto the Long Walk and was entered through an archway described as 'the largest to any Castle in England'. It led to the inner quadrangle.

Improvements were not confined to the Castle and its precincts. In May 1828 it was announced that there would be improvements to the streets to the west of the Castle including Castle Hill, Castle Street and Church Lane. These improvements included the removal of 'tumble down and poverty stricken hovels' to open up the vista between the Castle and the parish church. Also included in this slum clearance was the Queen Elizabeth Gateway at the top of Castle Street which was in a very poor state of repair.

On 9 December 1828 Jeffry Wyattville handed the King the master keys to his private apartments. Afterwards 'his Majesty was most graciously pleased to confer on him the honour of Knighthood'. The town also celebrated the King's return to this 'splendid abode of Royal magnificence' with a special dinner at the Town Hall hosted by the Mayor of Windsor where a loyal address was read out before it was later presented to the King. Although the King was in residence in his private apartments, work continued in the Castle. On 12 August 1829 between 300-400 men working on the Castle gathered on the North Terrace to give three cheers to his Majesty on the occasion of his birthday. The King provided a dinner for them at a number of nearby inns.

Once the King was in residence, the public were again admitted to the Castle and its terraces for the first time since the early 1820s. They were entertained by a band on the North Terrace. Visitors were able to visit St George's Hall, the state apartments and other parts of the Castle. However, works continued until the middle of the 1830s.(EK)

Princess Charlotte 1796 – 1817

Princess Charlotte was a regular visitor to Windsor. She enjoyed riding in Windsor Great Park and the company of her two favourite aunts who lived at the Castle. In 1812 she had her own establishment at Lower Lodge and in 1815 a larger establishment at Cranbourne Lodge. Both were in effect banishments from London after quarrels with her father, in 1812 over her visits to her mother, Caroline of Brunswick his estranged wife, and in 1815 the proposed marriage of Charlotte to the Prince of Orange.

In the newspaper's Court Circular we read that Princess's Charlotte's seventeenth birthday was celebrated at Frogmore in January 1913 with a party given by the Queen. The *Windsor Express* (December 1813) reported that

> Accompanied by the Queen and her father, Princess Elizabeth, the Duchess of Leeds and Miss [Cornelia] Knight went in two carriages from the castle to St. George's Chapel where Princess Charlotte was confirmed by the Archbishop of Canterbury, the Bishop of Salisbury and the Dean of Windsor. The following day she attended Divine Service at St. George's Chapel and received the sacrament.

During the visit of the Tsar of Russia to London in April 1814 to celebrate the defeat of Napoleon at Leipzig, Princess Charlotte had her first meeting with the impoverished Prince Leopold of Saxe-Coburg who had become a favourite with the Russian court. In February 1815 following their second meeting and with the support of the Prince Regent, a quiet marriage was celebrated at Carlton House, her father's London home, on 2 May 1816. After their honeymoon the newly weds-moved to their new home at Claremont in Esher.

The marriage had large public support and the news of Princess Charlotte's death on 6 November 1817 after giving birth to a still-born son was a shock for the whole nation. The *Windsor Express* was published with black borders round each page and declared that 'The death of Princess Charlotte has fallen upon the people like a sudden universal darkness'.

All the shops and inns were closed and every private house partially closed. Mourning garments were worn and markets closed early. All businesses were closed on the day of the funeral. Interment was to be in the royal vault in St George's Chapel where the west end and aisles were covered in black baize and the royal stalls hung with black cloth. Admission tickets for the public to the service were limited to the organ loft and aisles. There was a full description of the funeral in the newspaper which ended with a personal addition by Charles Knight Junior:

> On the morning of Tuesday I received from one of the Reverend Prebendaries of the College of Windsor, a ticket of admission to the Organ Loft of St. George's Chapel to witness the ceremonial of the late Princess Charlotte's internment. This I was given to understand was presented to me by the particular direction of the Dean and Chapter to allow me to make a faithful report of the solemnities and as a compliment to the office of chief magistrate which my father holds in the borough. At seven o'clock in the evening I claimed an entrance at the Outer Gate of the Lower Ward of the Castle, which was kept by two subalterns of the Foot Guards and a numerous body of rank and file. Constables of the Borough were also posted there but they were evidently treated as intruders upon these unconstitutional guardians of the public peace. I was roughly thrust back against the wheels of the carriages which were passing behind me; and told in common with many others, who, like myself had tickets, that no more would be admitted. For an hour I was buffeted about with my unfortunate companions, who comprised some of the most respectable inhabitants of Windsor, sometimes collared by the soldiers, sometimes jammed against the castle wall, and at all times insulted by dogmatical

assertions or sneering indifference. We at last retired in despair having rescued our lives till danger was no longer endurable. Ten minutes before the procession entered the gate I procured access to one of the officers under the escort of a sentinel; and having represented the peculiar circumstances under which I had obtained my ticket and the duty which I owed to the public to enforce my claim for admission, requested that the order of exclusion be withdrawn. I was haughtily repulsed. At this instant two military men with four ladies were passed through the gate without any authority than the dictum of the officer I was addressing. I complained of the unjust partiality in a respectful manner, for this presumption I was instantly handed over to the next corporal with orders to 'take back that man'. Collared like a felon I was forced along the line of foot guards, and on reaching the last soldier was thrust against a carriage like an intrusive hound.

Three months after the death of Princess Charlotte came the news that Sir Richard Croft, the leading obstetrician, who was brought in to assist the princess's regular physician, and had been criticised by many for his reluctance to use forceps during the labour had committed suicide. He fired two pistols simultaneously at his own head.

After the funeral a fund was started by the Duchess of York for a public memorial, raising £12,346. No one was allowed to give more than one shilling and the *Express* supported the appeal. This memorial was created by Matthew Wyatt and placed in the Urswick Chantry in the nave of St George's Chapel, Windsor Castle.

On the memorial the Princess's body lies covered by a shroud with only her hands just visible. Two female mourners draped in sheets weep on either side of her. Above the body is a sculpture of the Princess ascending to heaven, her face upturned towards the light, flanked by angels. One angel carries her infant son who also looks up to heaven.   (NO)

© Dean and Canons of St George's Chapel

Victoria

After the death of Princess Charlotte three royal Dukes married German princesses to try to produce an heir to the throne. The marriage in Germany of the Duke of Kent to the Princess Dowager of Leiningen was announced in the newspaper in June 1818. In July the ceremony was repeated at Kew Palace, together with the marriage of the Duke of Clarence to Princess Adelaide. The brides were given away by the Prince Regent.

Eleven months later the *Windsor and Eton Express* carried the news that the Duchess of Kent was safely delivered of a healthy female child on 24 May 1819 at Kensington Palace.

> 'The undersigned hereby certify, that her Royal Highness the Duchess of Kent was safely delivered of a female child, living, at a quarter past four o'clock in the morning of the 24th of May, 1819.
>
> 'DAVID D. DAVIS.
> 'J. WILSON, Domestic Physician to their Royal Highnesses.'

The Duke of Kent died in January 1820 at the age of 53. He had a severe cold and inflammation of the chest and had been bled three times and cupped twice. Was it the treatment or the inflammation that killed him? In his will he made his wife the sole guardian of his daughter Victoria. (March 1820)

Not much is reported in the paper about the young princess until February 1827, when an attendance at church in Kensington Palace with her mother and half-sister Feodore was worth a mention.

The following year Feodore, married Prince Hohenlohe of Laugenbourg at Kensington Palace. It was stressed that 'the bride and her royal sister, the Princess Victoria, were dressed entirely in articles of British manufacture; their dresses were of Buckinghamshire thread lace'.

In February 1829 the newspaper advertised prints of 'a highly finished portrait of Princess Victoria' by Anthony Steward for 5s; possibly to celebrate the princess's 10th birthday.

Royal Remains

Early in 1813 while workmen were creating a new royal mausoleum in St George's Chapel they accidentally broke through to the vault containing the body of Henry VIII, and there discovered the lead coffin of Charles I – with a lead scroll on top inscribed 'King Charles 1648' (*sic* – the King was executed in 1649, so this was probably the newspaper's error). No one had previously known where the King had been interred, hugger-mugger, after his execution, when the Cromwellians had forbidden a proper funeral. Charles II had ordered a search for his father's resting-place, but it had not been found.

When the news of this discovery reached the Prince Regent he was anxious that the coffin be opened in his presence, and attended with Sir Henry Halford, one of the physicians to George III. This investigation was kept secret at the time, but rumours got out and a hand-written note on the newspaper says that it took place on 1 April.

Workmen cut open part of the lead coffin from the head end, and found the body wrapped in a cerecloth. Sir Henry wrote a pamphlet describing the findings (reported 2 May 1813), telling how the winding sheet had been impregnated with an 'unctuous or greasy matter mixed with resin', to protect the body from decay. It was hard to release it from the head, but when it was done there must have been a sharp intake of breath as the face was revealed, 'apparently perfect as when he lived', and not just because it was identifiably the King's, but because the left eye was 'open and full'.

The head was lifted up: it had been severed by a single blow from the axe. The onlookers noted a full head of hair and a pointed beard, reddish in colour. This appeared to have been trimmed, perhaps to make the executioner's job easier or to provide the dead King's followers with keep-sakes. The head was then placed back on the shoulders of the corpse.

Henry VIII's lead coffin was also opened. It was in a poor state, seemingly 'beaten in by violence' (possibly by an explosion caused by the putrefaction of the body). Only a skull, with 'some hair on the chin', and the principal limb bones remained. The coffins of Jane Seymour, and a still-born child of Queen Anne were also found, but seem not to have been opened.

What Sir Henry's 1813 report doesn't reveal is that, not content with just viewing the remains of Charles I, he too wanted souvenirs and took away a piece of neck bone, a tooth and some hair. These were later given by Halford's son to the then Prince of Wales (later Edward VII), but in 1888 they were returned in a casket to lie on top of the coffin where they presumably still are. The 1813 investigators had also carelessly left King Charles's name-plate on Henry VIII's coffin, so it too was restored to its rightful place.

As a foot-note, the *Express* on 21 May 1826 recorded the sale for 100 guineas of the prayer-book used by Charles I at his execution. One wonders whether it was what it purported, and if so where it is now. (HD)

The sad story of the Camelopard

In June 1827 the newspaper reported that the Pasha of Egypt had presented King George IV with a camelopard for his menagerie in Windsor Park. Two weeks later more was revealed about this mysterious beast. Camelopard means 'beautiful animal' and is in fact a giraffe. The article stated that two babies were procured by shooting the mother, who was then taken to Egypt and eaten. The babies were offered to the Kings of France and England; unfortunately the one destined for England had since died. But all was not lost; the Pasha immediately got another giraffe which duly arrived in England in August, accompanied by two Egyptian cows to provide it with milk. The giraffe was said to drink 8-10 quarts of milk a day.

An article in the paper in December 1827 described the animal as very graceful, docile and gentle with a friendly disposition, even playful and not at all fearful. The writer observed that it had an awkward walk and noticed a deformed limb, which he put down to the treatment it had endured on the long journey from Sinaar to Cairo. The Arab traders had tied the poor animal to the back of one of the camels with tight ropes. This resulted in the injury from which it was never to recover.

For two months the giraffe was exhibited in London, and finally arrived at Sandpit Gate, Windsor Great Park at the end of October. The King gave permission for it to be seen on Saturdays and Mondays. The artist RB Davis made several paintings of the giraffe for the King, and even the fashion world went giraffe crazy. Female fashion for April 1828 included an evening dress of giraffe-coloured tiffany silk.

Sadly the deformed limb got worse. When the Duke of Cumberland and his son George visited it in May, the giraffe was held up in a sling and his knee was bathed with salt water. On 5 July 1828 the newspaper reported that 'little hope is entertained of the recovery of the giraffe, which cannot stand and has to be held up in a sling, but a dozen fine kangaroos arrived at the royal menagerie at Sandpit Gate'.

On 29 November this poem was printed in the newspaper:

FOR THE WINDSOR EXPRESS.

THE CAMELOPARD.

What plaint from the Forest, oh gale, dost thou bear?
Can sorrow be found in a region so fair?
From high palisades, or the folds of her tent,
Lone Echo has wafted the Giraffe's lament;
Beloved by a Monarch, ah who would not grieve,
A Lord so benign, so indulgent to leave!—
But Death, yet more potent, persists in his claim,
And langour pervades every nerve of her frame;
In hopeless dejection, extended she lies,
And thus to the Fawns, her attendants, she cries :—
" Ah! why was I brought from the desert afar,
To be followed and sought like a wandering star?
No creature in England e'er made such a talk,
Not even his Grace the Grand Falconer's Hawk!
Rank, talents, and beauty my levee await,
Ambassadors sometimes alight at my gate,
While Royalty deigns all my charms to admire,
Dividing his heart between me and Maria.
And oft though he comes his poor Giraffe to see,
Not one of his subjects is jealous of me.
They say that young truants from Eton will run,
To Peacocks, all tail, and tall Emews with none;
And laugh at the gait of the quaint Kangaroo,
Who, scorning four legs, hops away upon two;
But people of judgment and taste must prefer
A visit to me, though unable to stir.
Oh clime unpropitious—so misty and damp!
My eyes never close but I wake with the cramp.
In vain did the Arabs encircle my neck,
With words of dark import, all danger to check;
Ere long will the struggle of Nature be o'er,
And mine be the homage of Windsor no more.
In youth's early morning I'm summoned away,
From him who would gladly my journey delay;
No Lady from Egypt so dear to a Prince,
Save the famed Cleopatra some centuries since.
And you, gentle Fawns, who stand drooping around,
Like Charmian and Iras, in sorrow profound;
Oh weep not to see me, when stuffed and embalmed,
But think when your anguish by reason is calmed;
Your kindred at Cranbourne who rove in the chase,
From whence they are soon to be sent in disgrace,
Will envy my fate when they're destined to roam,
Like exiles of Parga, expelled from their home."

L. B.

The animal continued to deteriorate. Briefly in July 1829 it could stand on its own and the King was said to be delighted, but in April 1830 it died and was stuffed for posterity, but where is it now?

Trade and Commerce

The Demise of the Windsor Bank of Brown and Coombs

At the beginning of the nineteenth century Windsor had three banks. The oldest, founded by Richard Ramsbottom, a local brewer and Windsor MP in 1780, was called the Windsor Bank. In 1801 James Coombs, a local ironmonger established two banks, one also confusingly called the Windsor Bank and the other called the Windsor and Eton Bank; Coombs had a number of partners, the last one being Henry Brown.

Banks printed and issued their own notes, which were quite easy to forge. Until 1830 this was a capital offence.

Banknotes were issued to customers in return for silver or gold coins and the note would be validated by a signature and date. Each one would only be used a few times and was destroyed when it was returned to be cashed in.

The banks were legally bound to repay each note on demand. This is why there are so few used notes around today and the banknote here has survived because it was used as evidence during the trial of Brown and Coombs.

Bank note from the Windsor & Royal Borough Museum

Any rumour of a crisis would see customers rushing to the bank to reclaim their cash. 1816 saw the failure of a number of banks and other businesses. Brown and Coombs was among them, due partly to the dire economic situation, partly to bad management and partly the failure of Coombs' ironmongery business. The newspaper carried news of the failure of the bank in February 1816. Banknotes worth £17,789 were still in the hands of customers and could not be redeemed. Henry Brown and James Coombs were declared bankrupt and all their assets were seized. Creditors were asked to send in their accounts of demand to the White Hart Inn, where the initial inquiry took place.

In May all assets of James Coombs, including his houses and office in Church Street and Peascod Street were sold by auction. In July both Brown and Coombs were committed into custody at Newgate Prison for fraud, after appearing before the Commissioners of Bankrupts; they were accused of burning £17,000 in banknotes. In December 1817 they were declared bankrupt to the amount of £41,000, but the charges could not be substantiated and they were released.

Three years later, in May 1819 Henry Brown requested a hearing to clear his name but the Lord Chancellor refused.

The Windsor Savings Bank

The failure of the Windsor Bank caused much hardship among the thrifty labouring classes. The newspaper declared: 'many labouring persons who hold small sums have sustained the greatest losses'. Two lengthy articles appeared in the paper in February 1816 calling for the establishment of a savings bank in Windsor for 'people of either sex in the lower station of life'. In April, Earl Harcourt, one of Windsor's most prominent philanthropists, chaired a meeting at the Guildhall to discuss such a bank for Windsor and its neighbourhood. Present also were the Dean and Canons of Windsor, Provost and Fellows of Eton College, the Mayor and leading members of the town. The notice that the Savings Bank had been established with a reputable list of vice presidents, trustees and a management committee was published in May 1816. Earl Harcourt as president matched the King's donation of £20 to set up the bank.

Customers were cautious to begin with. When in July 1817 money was stolen from cottages in Bray, victims were told that they should have lodged their money in the Bank.

In July 1818 the newspaper informed the customers of the Savings Bank that interest had been added to their accounts, anyone wishing to receive his interest must make 'due application to the committee at the School-House on Monday between the hours of twelve and two'. In a letter to the editor the following year the writer pointed out that a number of customers had complained of being questioned when putting money in and lectured when withdrawing money.

However, in July 1820 when the half yearly account was published in the paper for the first time, a healthy balance was recorded. £2035 11s 4d had been deposited during the previous half year, and £1685 16s 10d withdrawn. There were 648 depositors divided into social classes with a turnover of over eleven thousand:

By 1828 the turnover of the Savings Bank had gone up to £38,612 1s 10d.

Wife selling

Wife selling was not an uncommon practice in days when divorce was impossible for poor people. Often these sales were a convenient arrangement between husband, wife and lover.

In September 1815 a wife was offered for sale at the King's Head Inn in Staines. 'There was a very numerous attendance to witness this singular sale, ... only 3s 4d was offered for the lot, no one choosing to contend with the bidder for the fair object'. The purchaser was said to have a 'long and intimate acquaintance with the fair object'.

Selling a Wife by Rowlandson

Another wife sale was reported in March 1817. Changing attitudes to the practice were reflected in the tone of the reporters: 'That most scandalous and disgraceful practice of selling a wife with a halter round her neck, was witnessed on Saturday last in the public market place of Kingston-upon-Thames. The husband bought a new halter for 15d with which he led his fair rib to the Town-hall, and having paid 2d for the toll or right of selling, she was knocked down to a countryman at the price of 1s.' Questions were asked why the magistrate did not intervene.

Wife selling was not an illegal practice until the 20th century, but was increasingly frowned upon. Some local magistrates often took the law into their own hands and made arrests, as this mention of wife selling shows. In November 1817 under the heading of 'A Disgraceful Transaction', it reported that a woman was sold at Andover market with a halter round her neck for 2s 6d. Both seller and purchaser were arrested.

But twice more did the paper report on wife selling during this period. In January 1824 a man sold his wife for 10s at Chipping Ongar market after paying 1d toll, the customary charge for live-stock, and in December 1827 a labourer tried to sell his wife at Windsor market. They had to leave in a hurry when they were threatened with imprisonment.

Public Transport

MESSRS. MOODY, LILLEWHITE and Co. Respectfully acquaint their Friends and the Public, that their EARLY COACH will Start on TUESDAY MORNING next, at SIX O'CLOCK, and continue at the same Hour during the Summer Season.

A COACH, through EGHAM, STAINES, and ENGLEFIELD GREEN, every Morning at Seven o'Clock; which calls coming in and going out at the New Inn, Windsor, and leaves London at 4 o'Clock.

Likewise Coaches at Nine o'Clock and Three, as usual.

From the mid eighteenth century, turnpike roads had 'facilitated more rapid and efficient transportation' of goods and people, and from 1784 mail-coaches ran the length and breath of Britain. During the early nineteenth century, this was still the only way to travel great distances.

In June 1816 the Royal Union Post Coaches introduced early morning coaches to London, leaving Windsor at 6am, returning from Piccadilly at 4pm, 'due to popular demand'. In 1818 Henry Thumwood took over the Royal Union Coaches and introduced three Post Coaches to London a day.

A number of private coach companies started advertising in the *Windsor and Eton Express* once the war with France was over, and new services were announced regularly. Some only operated a summer season. In April 1815 a new 'Elegant Post Coach' carrying four inside ran from Windsor to Ludgate Inn, London, via Englefield Green and Staines, leaving the Crown Inn Windsor at 7am each morning and returning at 4pm except Sundays.

Prices varied from 7s to 14s inside, and 1s to 4s outside. The most expensive was Henry Thumwood's new summer season service from Windsor to Brighton, which started in April 1825; he charged £1.0s.6d inside and 14s outside. During Ascot week coaches left from the Swan Inn Windsor and the Christopher Inn in Eton three times a day.

Most coaches carried four or six inside and a maximum of 12 outside, but in September 1814 the Reading to London coach company was charged with carrying 21 passengers outside instead of 12.

Travelling by stage-coach was not without danger, accidents were frequently reported in the press. Coaches often overturned, especially if they were overcrowded like the Reading coach. In June 1813 a passenger was killed when he fell off the Bath coach. He and his two sisters were on their way to London to pick up a legacy of £50 each. In October 1818 the Bath coach overturned near Langley when the horses took fright at some donkeys; several passengers suffered broken bones, including the footman of Prince Leopold (Princess Charlotte's widower). He had two broken legs and a dislocated shoulder. When the axle broke on the Windsor to London coach in June 1816 going at 7 mph, one passenger was killed as he jumped off the coach.

The other hazard was highway robbery, although notorious highwaymen like Dick Turpin were becoming a thing of the past. In February 1829 an attempt to rob one of the Windsor coaches by men on horseback, riding behind and trying to force the boot was prevented by the coachman as 'he cut them right and left with his whip'.

In May 1814 a considerable amount of money belonging to Windsor bankers Messrs Ramsbottom was taken from the Hertford coach. The cheeky thieves posted drafts and cheques back to the bank as they were no use to them. In August a suspect was apprehended with £40 in notes; altogether £5,348 2d had been stolen. Another large sum of money, £1,900 in Windsor bank notes, was stolen in 1815. In December 1820 the Windsor to London coach was robbed of a suitcase, a basket of fish and a buttock of beef. In December 1818, thieves took advantage of thick fog by stealing several parcels from the Windsor coach.

Stage coaches could take between three and four hours from Windsor to London, post coaches were a little faster, but in March 1826 William Goodchild promised that the 'new, elegant and light' Tally Ho! Post Coach would take you to London in 2½ hours, which would have been faster than Moody's coaches. In September 1826, a man running alongside one of Moody's Windsor coaches wearing only a flannel jacket and pantaloons, kept up with it all the way.

But there were signs of changes to come during this period. In September 1828 the newspaper reported that a man called Walker from Berkshire had invented a mechanical steam carriage, 'which will go at 12 mph'.

Caleys

The whole history of the firm of Caley's can be followed in the pages of the *Windsor Express* from before they took number 19 High Street, Windsor, until the store closed in 2006. The first advertisement, on the front page in 1813, tells us that Maria Caley left her own workshop in Thames Street to join her sister Mrs Charlotte Noke, in Castle Street (now Castle Hill). She advertised for an apprentice several times.

M. CALEY,

Milliner, Dress-Maker, and Haberdasher,

LATE OF THAMES-STREET, WINDSOR,

BEGS Leave to inform the Ladies of Windsor, Eton, and their Environs, that the above Business will in future be carried on in Castle-Street, in conjunction with her Sister, Mrs. NOKE.

M. C. takes this Opportunity of returning her most grateful Thanks for the numerous and distinguished Favors hitherto so liberally conferred; and (jointly with her Sister) most respectfully solicits a Continuance of the same.

Maria Caley's brother John married Mary Ann Goodman in Stamford in 1820; the *Stamford Mercury* recorded the event, but not the *Windsor Express*. Because there was no record of the marriage in Windsor various rumours arose. One of them credited Maria with a Royal Warrant and another was that she was called Mrs Caley as a mark of respect. Neither of these rumours was true. Perhaps it is unfortunate that both women had a first initial M.

Three weeks after her marriage Mary Ann Caley was advertising her services as a milliner from the Castle Street address in Windsor with a Royal Warrant at the top of the advertisement. It was she who had been awarded the Warrant by Queen Charlotte. John and Mary Ann advertised regularly and John's notification of his removal to premises 'opposite the Town-hall' on 5 April 1823 marks the beginning of 183 years in the same place.

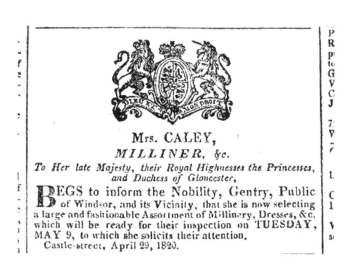

Mrs. CALEY,
MILLINER, &c.
To Her late Majesty, their Royal Highnesses the Princesses, and Duchess of Gloucester,

BEGS to inform the Nobility, Gentry, Public of Windsor, and its Vicinity, that she is now selecting a large and fashionable Assortment of Millinery, Dresses, &c. which will be ready for their inspection on TUESDAY, MAY 9, to which she solicits their attention,
Castle-street, April 29, 1820.

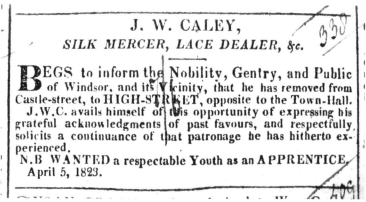

J. W. CALEY,
SILK MERCER, LACE DEALER, &c.

BEGS to inform the Nobility, Gentry, and Public of Windsor, and its Vicinity, that he has removed from Castle-street, to HIGH-STREET, opposite to the Town-Hall. J.W.C. avails himself of this opportunity of expressing his grateful acknowledgments of past favours, and respectfully solicits a continuance of that patronage he has hitherto experienced.
N.B WANTED a respectable Youth as an APPRENTICE, April 5, 1823.

One month after their move to the High Street there was a fire in Castle Street and their former premises were badly damaged. The description of the fire in the *Express* enables us to identify exactly where the Castle Street shop was. John Caley and 'Inmates at Mr Caleys' are listed amongst the names on the subscription list to help those who had lost their businesses. John gave £1 and the inmates gave 18s.

season.

BIRTH.

On Saturday last, at Titness-park, Sunning-hill, Berks, the lady of the Right Hon. Lord Gavagh, of a son.

MARRIED.

On Saturday last, at All Souls' Church, St. Marylebone, Sir Montague Cholmeley, Bart. M.P. of Easton hall, Lincolnshire, to Catherine, fourth daughter of Benj. Way, Esq. of Denham-park, Bucks.

On Tuesday last, at Windsor, by the Rev. I. Gosset, Mr. Wm. Goodman, of Louth, Lincoln, to Maria, youngest daughter of Mr. Caley, of Frogmore.

DIED.

On Sunday last, at Thatcham, Berks, aged 41 years, Thomas Hedges, Esq.

We hear nothing more of Maria until the announcement of her marriage to William Goodman, her brother-in-law, in 1826. The couple later set up a business in Uxbridge doing the same work as the Caleys of Windsor and advertising in the *Express*; the classifieds often appeared together on the front page and offering very similar merchandise.

MRS. CALEY,
MILLINER, &c. TO THE ROYAL FAMILY,

BEGS respectfully to inform the Ladies of Windsor and its vicinity, that she purposes having ready for their inspection her NEWLY SELECTED MILLINERY, DRESSES, &c. on TUESDAY, MAY the 5th.

N.B.—Tuscan, Leghorn, Chip and Straw Bonnets, Stays, Baby Linen, &c.

Two or three APPRENTICES wanted.

SPRING FASHIONS.

MRS. GOODMAN respectfully informs the Ladies of Uxbridge, and its vicinity, that she has had selected from the first houses in London, a genteel and fashionable Assortment of Millinery, Dresses, Pelisses, Leghorn and Straw Bonnets, Baby Linen, Stays, Flowers, &c. for their inspection on Friday, May 8th, to which she solicits their attention.

Mr. G. will also have a variety of Silks, of the newest colours, Printed Muslins, Shawls, &c.

Uxbridge, May 1st, 1829.

Maria died in 1834, shortly after giving birth to her fifth child. The notice was clearly written by her devastated husband. (PM)

On the 8th instant, after a few days' illness, Maria, the beloved wife of Mr. Goodman, of Uxbridge, leaving four children (two of whom are in arms) to lament their irreparable loss.

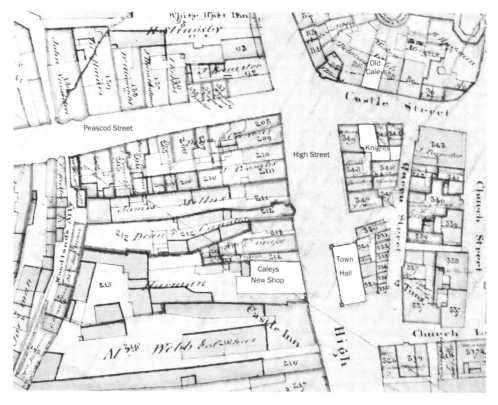

*Part of a Windsor Map of about 1810 showing Caleys original premises
opposite Knight's Bookshop and their new premises opposite the Town Hall*

Breweries and brewing

Three breweries were regularly mentioned in the newspaper, Messrs
Ramsbottom & Legh in Thames Street, Messrs Jennings of Jennings Yard and
J&F Twinch of Peascod Street.

John Ramsbottom Sr with his partner James Baverstock had bought the
brewery from Henry Isherwood in 1780. After the death of Ramsbottom Sr at
his residence in Thames Street at the age of 82 in April 1826, the brewery
continued and expanded under the name of Messrs Ramsbottom and Legh,
with his son John Ramsbottom, in charge. John Jr also led the bank of
Ramsbottom, Baverstock and Co and had taken on his uncle Richard's mantle
as MP for Windsor. In November 1828 the brewery installed a new patent
furnace 'to consume the smoke of one of their large brewing coppers ... with a
view to diminish the annoyance to their immediate neighbourhood'

68

Thomas Jennings was first mentioned in January 1813 when Robert Rose publicly apologised for destroying a brewer's cask. This is an odd news item and perhaps it signifies how important beer and brewing was. In March 1815 Thomas Haydon stole beer from Messrs Jennings for which he was sentenced to death. However, he was given a royal pardon by the Prince of Wales for 'exemplary conduct' in gaol. J&F Twinch first appeared in the *Express* when they informed the readers in November 1819, that they had commenced the brewing of ale.

Beer was very important, even children were given small beer to drink rather than water, which was generally polluted. The rise of the price of porter from 3d a quart to 6d in 1815 persuaded many to drink spirits. A letter to the editor of the *Express* in June 1815 complained about the high price of beer in Windsor which at 6d a quart 'is 1d dearer than in London'. The writer said that he had a wife and two sons and 'we contrive to indulge ourselves in the luxury of two quarts of beer a day', but he only earned £3 a month. He will not have been pleased when the price of porter rose by ½d in 1816, because of the rising price of malt and hops. Even before this increase, there was concern about the large number of 'gin shops' following the rise of beer prices.

The government hoped the introduction of the 'Beer Bill' in 1823 would solve the problem and 'encourage the consumption of beer rather than sprits'. This bill allowed beer to be sold in unlicensed premises in small quantities for 3d a quart. Immediately dozens of beer houses sprang up in Windsor.

But there also was much concern about the quality of the beer. In March 1818 a petition of Reading silk-weavers, complaining about the high price and poor quality of beer, was signed by 14,000 people.

A long article in the *Express* in October 1827 praised the virtues of drinking beer rather than wine or spirits:

> Good home-brewed beer has been styled by some *vinum Britannicum* and by others *liquid bread.* There can be no doubt of its highly nutritive and wholesome qualities, and it is much to be regretted, that so few families in this kingdom now ever brew their own beer.

The majority of families, especially working families did not have the facilities to brew their own beer. However, looking at house sales, you find that larger houses were equipped with their own brew-houses. A large residence in High Street, with gardens to Bachelors' Acre, for sale in March

1828 had its own brew-house. Baylis House in Slough also listed a brew-house when it came up for sale in November 1820 and servants needed the know-how of brewing:

> Wanted, a steady, active, single man 30-40 years old, must understand the care of horse and chaise and have a knowledge of brewing.
> (Oct 1826)

Breweries continued to flourish in Windsor during the nineteenth century. There were five of them by the 1860s, but during the twentieth century they closed one by one. Today we again have a small brewery on the Vansittart Estate, called Windsor & Eton Brewery producing special beers and ales.

Chimney sweeps

The first mention of chimney-sweepers in the *Express* was in July 1816. It was taken from a report of the Middlesex Sessions. William Moles, master sweeper, was acquitted of the murder of his 5-year-old apprentice, John Hewlings, although a number of witnesses gave the most harrowing accounts of the violence used against the small boy. However, he was sentenced to two years imprisonment for brutally treating the child.

During 1817 there were a number of meetings and petitions to Parliament to consider the best way to abolish climbing boys. Liberal MP Mr Bennet moved to bring in a Bill in the House of Commons in February 1818 to prevent climbing boys under the age of 14, and In November 1818 the House of Lords debated if chimneys could be swept without climbing boys. The opinion was that machinery, which had recently been developed, was not good enough and climbing boys could not be dispensed with. The suggestion of using geese, as they did in some parts of Ireland where geese are dragged up chimneys by their neck, was rejected as being inhuman!

In September 1822 the *Express* highlighted the plight of the climbing boys with this article:

> We have long noticed, and with considerable pain, the lamentable and disgraceful state of the chimney-sweepers of this borough. In common with many of those who feel that no part of the human species should be brutalized by their habitual occupations, we have regretted that a more strenuous effort has not been made altogether to abolish climbing boys by the use of machinery...The chimney-sweepers of Windsor are never cleansed or decently clothed on the Sabbath-day. They are consequently deprived of comforts which belong once a week to the

children of the most humble. They are completely shut out from social life; their enjoyments are of the very lowest cast: their lives are one unvarying round of labour and pain, and filth, and disease. ...Add to this, a large portion of the climbing children of Windsor are females. We trust that these observations will call the attention of our worthy Magistrate...'

It took three years for the 'worthy Magistrate' to respond. In August 1825 the paper reported:

We are glad that our worthy Mayor has taken the subject of the climbing boys into consideration. The master chimney-sweepers have been summoned before him, and complaints having been made as to the pitiable condition of their boys, a pledge was given by them that their comforts and wants should be strictly attended to. We hope, in future, that we shall not see them, on a day when the meanest workman assumes a decent appearance, clad in the sooty habiliment of their trade.

Meanwhile the paper continued to report incidences of cruel treatment of climbing boys, like the little lad who choked to death in a chimney in Mortimer Street, London in March 1821, or the case of John Holgate of York, who in August 1827 was found not guilty of murder after his climbing-boy died when Holgate put soot on the fire 'to smoke him out.'

The last word on climbing boys in this run of the newspaper was in December 1829. A London magistrate refused to allow the Overseer of the Poor for St Martin-in-the-Field to apprentice two orphan boys aged six and seven, in a trade 'so revolting to every feeling of humanity'.

The Slave Trade

The British government had abolished the slave trade in March 1807, but this did not mean that other European countries toed the line. The first mention in the *Express* was in September 1814, with an article on the trade, which was still carried on under the Spanish and Portuguese flags. In June that year the Freemasons, chaired by the Duke of Gloucester discussed the abolition of the slave trade, and petitions were sent to Parliament on the subject in July 1814. Concern was expressed in the newspaper when in September it was reported that France was again trading with slaves to St Domingo. In October 1814 the *Express* revealed that France and Portugal had been granted five years in which to continue the trade. In June 1815, Mr Wilberforce moved to prevent the clandestine importation of slaves into the

West Indies and a year later, he asked what had been done to enforce abolition.

The first international breakthrough came in 1818, when the Netherlands agreed to abolish the African slave trade in a treaty with Britain (reported in the newspaper in May 1818). This treaty was also ratified with Spain in 1823, but not with Portugal, after two Spanish vessels with 450 slaves were taken by British ships off the coast of Africa in 1821.

British ships continued to capture French and Portuguese slavers and liberated the slaves, as reported in an article in August 1824. Those who were involved in the trade were brought to justice. In January 1820, two foreigners, J A Carrol and A Vilemont were found guilty at the Old Bailey of shipping 200 slaves to Mauritius from Madagascar. They were sentenced to 14 years transportation.

The Slaves

The first of the great rebellions of the West Indies broke out in Barbados in April 1816; it was reported in the *Express* in June under 'Negro Insurrection'. Martial Law was proclaimed and the 'militia has been unremittingly employed in conjunction with the King's troops here, in putting down this alarming rebellion'. The report had a presentiment of things to come: 'This is the first instance of perhaps many yet to come of the fatal tendency to the peace and security of those islands'. Not until eight years later were the slaves of Barbados granted some amelioration of their condition, one of which was the right to religious instruction, another the right to leisure time (December 1823).

Missionaries were looked upon with suspicion; John Smith was tried in 1824 in Demerara for producing discontent in negro slaves against their masters. The trial, which according to the newspaper 'proves nothing against Mr Smith, [is] valuable as to throwing light on the slave-system of the colonies' (March 1824).

Another rebellion in Jamaica in September 1824 ended with the ringleaders in court, condemned to be hanged 'for the purpose of obtaining your freedom by force'.

Meanwhile at home, former slaves had access to British law, but not always to British justice. Philip Thompson, a black man bought as a slave in Jamaica by a Mrs Storer, complained of beatings and ill treatment. Mrs Storer was found not guilty at Reading assizes. (March 1825)

The Slavery Abolition Act was passed in 1833, which freed all slaves in British colonies.

Lighting the Streets of Windsor

The Commissioners of the pavements for Windsor were responsible for lighting the lamps of the Borough. They contracted out the duties of a lamplighter each year. The number of lamps in Windsor was not given, but Maidenhead had 110 of them. Damage to the lamps was a serious offence. In May 1822, two men convicted of 'wilfully breaking and injuring' a number of lamp irons were fined £17 16s.

The lamps were filled with sperm oil and lit only the main roads in Windsor. In September 1824 new lamps were erected on the road from the Royal Lodge to Bishopsgate and Cumberland Lodge. But the days of the lamplighters were nearly over.

Roadside gas-lights had been installed in London in 1825, but it was not until March 1827 that a meeting was called in Windsor to discuss the possibility of lighting the town with gas lamps; the proposal was supported by the King. The Windsor Gas Light Company was set up and shares were offered at £20 each. In September the shareholders met at the Guildhall to discuss whether to use coal gas, or that produced by oil or resin. They came down in favour of resin. Land was procured in the Goswells for the gas works in November 1827. Finally in August of the following year:

> The Gas Committee commenced lighting up on Saturday evening, to the gratification of the whole town, and to the extacy [sic] of the little boys and girls, who greeted the torch-bearer with rounds of applause for every successive light which he conjured into existence. At present the line of lights commences at Windsor Bridge, continues along Thames-street and High-street, and reaches as far as Frogmore.

An explosion at the gas works in November 1828, which destroyed 2cwt of resin and shattered nearly all the windows in the building, was a serious setback, and so was a failure of the gas supply in March 1829 which blacked out Windsor. Queen Adelaide refused to have resin gas in Windsor Castle when she moved in, in July 1830. The problem was not solved until the gas company changed over to a less volatile coal gas in October 1830, which they re-assured everyone, was 'a safe, cheap and powerful light suitable for private dwellings'.

Leisure

The Theatre Royal

In the very first issue of the paper the managers of the Theatre Royal, Messrs Jonas and Penley, announced the summer season of plays at the Theatre Royal, beginning with *Macbeth*. They declared that 'they have spared neither Pains or Expence in providing a company from the Theatre Royal London'. The performances were staged in Windsor's pocket-handkerchief of a playhouse close by the parish church, which dated from the 1790s when King George III was an enthusiastic playgoer.

With their dramatic plots, visual spectacle and skilful acting, plays provided good entertainment for the town of Windsor. But there were many who disapproved of the theatre and such was the fear of corruption of the young (through plots of sexual attraction and the occasional glimpse of an actress in tights), and such the power of Eton College, that the theatre was only licensed to open when the boys were on holiday.

But for those who had no insuperable moral scruples, including Charles Knight Jr who loved the theatre, there was the chance to see good plays and fine players. Performances were always announced in the paper (and tickets, usually ranging in price from one to four shillings, could be obtained from the newspaper offices). Not all productions were traditional: a woman, Jane Powell (in tights), played the Prince in *Hamlet* to acclaim in August 1812. The greatest tragic actress of the age, Sarah Siddons, appeared, albeit in a comedy, in Sheridan's popular *The School for Scandal* (1777) in January 1813, while the finest comic actress, Dora Jordan, came to Windsor that summer. The evening's entertainment always included two plays, a 'main piece' plus a comic 'afterpiece', and for good measure songs, dances and novelty items such as (5 September 1813) a hornpipe danced 'blindfolded over 12 eggs'.

Then in 1814 the lease on the theatre was up, and the building became instead a respectable dissenting chapel.

But there were still plenty who wanted a theatre for Windsor, and quickly a subscription list was got up under Charles Knight's leadership. A purpose-built theatre was commissioned on the site where the current Theatre Royal stands. Professionals from London came to paint the decorations and scenery, and on the 6 August 1815 the *Express* triumphantly announced:

On Monday, August 21st, 1815
Under the Management of
Messrs Jonas and Penley;
When will be performed, the celebrated comedy of
The School for Scandal
Previous to the Play
An Occasional address
Written by Mr. C. Knight
And to be Spoken by Mrs S. Penley of the Theatre
Royal, Drury Lane.
End of the Play, a favourite SONG by Mrs Margerum
To conclude with the Farce of
The Sleep Walker
Boxes 4s – Pit 2s –
Gallery 1s
Doors to be opened at Six, and to begin at Seven O'Clock.
No person can be admitted behind the Scenes.

Knight's 'address', printed in the paper, tackled the issue of supposed moral decadence in the theatre and began by asking

Where shall the Muses fly, in this cold age
When Hood-wink'd Zeal proscribes the graceful stage;
Thrusts out the Drama from its wonted seat;
Nor leaves to us* the privilege to eat? [*The Actors*]
Say, would not Dullness' self in rage bestir her,
To see gay comedy dismiss'd the *Borough*?
Who would not call poetic Vengeance down
On those who forc'd the Tragic Maid from Town?

At the conclusion of his verses he called for three cheers for the newly-launched theatre, and it was no doubt a satisfaction to be able to report after the last play of the summer season that an audience 'so large and respectable was never before witnessed in the Borough' (17 September 1815). The play was Garrick and Colman's comedy of 1776, *The Clandestine Marriage*, with a very funny plot centring round Fanny, who has secretly married her father's clerk but dare not confess it despite the attentions of two other suitors.

Year on year thereafter the theatre opened for a summer and winter season, and for Ascot week. Programmes were always announced in the paper and unlike today every evening offered a different one. A typical evening in 1816, for example, started with George Lillo's play of 1731 which they named *the Tragedy of George Barnwell* though its full title is *The London Merchant or the History of George Barnwell*, a tale of a profligate young man who robs and murders his uncle to fund his life-style: it could hardly be faulted by the Windsor righteous for its severe moral lesson as Barnwell and his mistress go to the gallows. After the tragedy the audience could relax with a comic song, a ballet, and then a farce called *Fortune's Frolic.* Playgoers got full value for their money though the managers were restricted in the profits they could make by the conditions of opening.

Edmund Kean as Hamlet

Mrs MARDYN.
as
MISS PEGGY.

There were occasional star performances which drew big audiences, notably when the great tragedian Edmund Kean played such classic Shakespearean roles as Othello, Richard III and Hamlet, though he once failed to turn up for *Hamlet.* For such appearances by celebrities prices could be raised, as for the performances by Mrs [Mary] Mardyn, known for her portrayal of lively young women, in 1816.

To celebrate the coronation of George IV in 1821 the first performance of the summer season was free! Unlike George III's time royalty did not now often patronise the theatre, though Princess Augusta sometimes sponsored a performance. From time to time the theatre was opened outside the seasons for concerts by military bands (officers were also frequent sponsors of performances), or for the popular lectures on astronomy by a DF Walker whose demonstrations made use of a 'large transparent orrery' called an *Eidouranion*. An Indian juggler, Khia Kwan Kruse, performed in March 1824, and later that year an infant prodigy, six-year-old Master Roscius Grossmith from Reading, gave 'three evenings of entertainments of humorous descriptions, imitations and songs'. His true first names were William Robert, and he had an astonishing repertoire, including big Shakespearian roles and performing *all* the parts in a comedy (he would become the uncle of brothers George and Weedon Grossmith who wrote *The Diary of A Nobody*). The awestruck newspaper reporter stated that his 'talents exceed anything we have ever before witnessed' and children and schools were admitted at half-price.

The theatre could be ambitious and in 1826 staged several performances of what must have been a difficult and expensive production, Weber's opera of 1821 *Der Freischutz* ('The Freeshooter'). It is a blend of romance and Gothic horror, which though not often performed in this country today was popular then, its most striking scene set in the 'Wolf's Glen', with apparitions and an appearance by the devil.

Audiences were generally appreciative but intriguingly, in the previous year (27 August 1825) the front page of the newspaper printed a public apology:

> Whereas I, John Hexell, did on the evening of Tuesday last, cause a disturbance at the Theatre by throwing an Onion at Mr S. Bennett when performing on stage, thereby subjecting myself in a prosecution; and Mr Penley having kindly agreed to forego any further proceedings, on condition of my publicly apologising and paying the costs thereof, I do hereby humbly ask pardon of the said Mr S. Bennett, and of the Audience generally.

Sadly we are not told any more – why did he throw an onion at a performer?

Worse trouble was reported on 4 July 1829 during the Ascot season. A group of officers of the 2nd Life Guards had taken a box when one of them, seeing a playbill floating down from the Gallery, leaned over and with his whip attempted to strike or catch it. But he missed the bill, catching instead the bonnet of a 'female' sitting below in the pit. 'The female's husband took umbrage at the affront', and with the support of others launched an attack on the soldiers, aiming to eject them from their box. There then ensued 'a disgraceful uproar', before calm was restored.

The summer season continued peacefully, ending with George Farquhar's 1702 comedy *The Inconstant or The Way to Win Him* (Farquhar is best-known today for *The Recruiting Officer*) and an afterpiece *The Vampire*, which no doubt sent playgoers home with suitably chilled spines. Year in and year out the theatre would continue to provide pleasure and entertainment until a fire in 1908 forced a further rebuilding. (HD)

Hunting

Hunting was a major pastime of the rich and well-connected during the nineteenth century, and the Royal Hunt was regularly reported in the local press. It was not only in Windsor Forest where the hunt roamed, but huntsmen could set off from Bracknell, Winkfield Plains, Burnham, Slough etc. Often the quarry was chased through the centre of Windsor. A stag or deer was released from a cart and the huntsmen and hounds followed after giving the animal a little time to get away. Once caught, it was taken back to the compound for another day's sport. The distances these hunts covered are amazing. In October 1813 the Royal Hunt pursued a deer from Bagshot, through Winkfied, St Leonards, into Clewer where it swam across the Thames to the amusement of the crowd. It then made its way through Eton College to Salt Hill and was finally cornered in a lane in Stoke.

One of the longest hunts reported was in November 1816:

> The Prince Regents Stag Hounds met at Two Mile -Brook, near Salthill, when a most beautiful deer was uncarted for the amusement of more than a hundred horsemen, he was remarked by all to be the finest, and in condition superior to any other ever seen.

The stag was released into a small cover and went 'by East Burnham to Farnham, through Black Park, over Iver Heath to Uxbridge and Cowley, leaving Hayes to the left, by Southhill, crossed the Grand Junction and left Brentford to the right, then crossed the county near Tyburn Turnpike, and away to Ealing, thence to Acton, and over Wormwood Scrubs to Hodesden, where he was taken, after four hours and a half of as good hunting as ever was seen'. The chase was in excess of 40 miles.

One Stag went shopping in Eton:

A November hunt in 1820, which started in Stoke Common followed the stag through Slough, Datchet to Eton and Windsor, crossing the Thames twice. In Eton it took refuge in the house of Mr Castles the pork butcher, but made a quick exit 'with a cur dog on his heels'. After a dash over Windsor Bridge it climbed the 100 steps. The huntsmen rode round into the Castle to meet the deer at the top, but it fooled them and turned back towards Eton College and into the shop of Mr Levy the orange merchant, where it stayed in the kitchen for some time. After exiting at the rear of the house it was finally taken trying to leap over the wall between Eton College and Fifteen-arch Bridge.

Another hunt went through the centre of Windsor in October 1822:

On Monday the Royal Hunt was well attended with company of all ranks. A fine deer was turned out of the cart at King's Beech Hill, soon after ten o'clock, for the day's diversion. The deer showed great sport, taking across the Heath towards Hatchet-lane, through the inclosure by Winkfield Plain and St. Leonard's-hill, running with great swiftness by the Spital barracks into Windsor, where he ran up Peascod-street, the hounds being close up with him, to the great amusement of the spectators. He took to the right into the Sun-passage, which is very narrow, but was met by two working-men, who made him turn round, and come back again into the street. He crossed the street, and ran down Mr George's passage, and leaped over the high paling into the Goswells, where he crossed the Thames to the left of Windsor. The huntsmen and hounds, with a numerous field of sportsmen, went over Windsor ferry, and renewed the chase the other side of Eton College, the deer taking across the fields of Dorney common, towards the Bath Road, where he was taken, after a chase of upwards of two hours and a half hard running.

Hunts did not always go to plan. In December 1820 one poor animal was chased from Farnham Common through Slough and Datchet to Windsor, where it tried to jump into the Castle grounds, but died impaled on railings in front of the Castle wall.

In July 1821 tragedy struck the King's hounds. When signs of rabies appeared in the pack, they were sent to Brighton to be washed daily in the sea 'which has unfortunately, proved ineffectual'. The whole pack had to be destroyed.

But woe-betide anyone who tried to poach the Royal game. With poor harvests, widespread unemployment and starvation, helping yourself to game from Windsor Forest was a tempting option. In the process gamekeepers and poachers often confronted each other. In February 1814 two gamekeepers were attacked and beaten by five poachers; only one was caught and prosecuted, and although a £50 reward was offered for the apprehension of the others, there was no report of their capture in the paper. In August 1818 Mr Cox the gamekeeper was murdered by poachers who again seem to have got away. But three poachers from Sunningdale who attacked and 'ill-treated' a gamekeeper in March 1828 were caught, sentenced to death and executed at Reading later the same month. Most poachers though were fined up to £50, sent to prison or transported to New South Wales for seven years. However, a gamekeeper who shot a poacher usually got away with it. In October 1815 George Vansittart's gamekeeper George Smith shot and killed poacher Joseph Bishop in Bisham Wood. The verdict was justifiable homicide.

One way of deterring poachers was by setting man-traps and spring-guns. These were first mentioned in the paper in March 1813:

> In consequence of the daring Outrages lately committed in this Park, on the Persons of his Royal Highness the Prince Regent's Assistant Gamekeeper, and the incalculable destruction of the Game by a Gang of lawless and desperate POACHERS, who for some time past have infested the Park; it has been deemed expedient to adopt strong measures to prevent if possible, a recurrence of such scandalous practices'.

But man-traps could and did endanger innocent people. A poor old woman gathering sticks in Bisham Wood fell into a pit-trap, sustaining dangerous injuries. George Vansittart, the owner of the wood, visited her and reported that she was quite fit and well (March 1817).

Sport

One of the major features of any newspaper today is the sports page, or indeed sports pages at the back of the paper. The *Windsor and Eton Express* of the nineteenth century did not have a sports page, but sporting events were regularly reported and commented on. We find reports on cricket matches, foot races, horse races, rowing and boxing sandwiched between general articles but there were also mentions of bull baiting and fights between lions and mastiffs; although they attracted huge purses, there was already a movement against cruel sports. In a letter to the paper in November 1814 a reader asked for an end to the Bull-Bait in Windsor.

Boxing

Bare knuckle fighting about 1820

Boxing [bare knuckle fighting] seems to have been extremely popular and could bring you great wealth, but it was also very dangerous and often led to serious injuries, even the death of one of the combatants and a charge of manslaughter. In February 1813 a boxing match in Beach-hill, Berkshire was fought between George Humphrey, a coachman and John Harlington, a waterman for twenty guineas. The reporter said that after fighting for just ten minutes 'both were so much punished about the head, that their features were not distinguishable'. Even so, they carried on for one more hour.

A boxing match at the Coach and Horses in Maidenhead Thicket in May 1818 to settle a quarrel between Stephen Pigott and Mr Charlton resulted in Pigott's death, Charlton was committed for manslaughter. This may not have been a prize fight but in July 1825, several boxing contests took place at Knowle Hill near Maidenhead with stakes of £400.

Betting on boxing matches also caused casualties. In May 1823 the paper reported on the suicide of Thomas Elliott, a young gentleman of a large fortune, who shot himself after losing several thousand pounds betting on boxing matches.

Sometimes emotions took over; a boxing match in a field at Hay near Uxbridge in March 1817 between Scroggins and Turner attracted over 20,000 people. The bets were declared null and void after one hour's fighting, as the ropes were trampled under foot and the contest became a street fight.

Cricket

Cricket was a popular game, regularly reported in the *Express*. The origins of the word 'cricket' are not known, but the first recorded reference to it comes in the sixteenth century; by the early nineteenth century the rules were laid down as we now know them. Though there are no women's games recorded in Windsor, girls played cricket too: when they were children Princess Augusta enjoyed playing with her brothers.

Games were played on Bachelors' Acre, the Brocas, or sometimes in the Great Park. The first to appear in the paper was a match on the Brocas between 'eleven gentlemen of Sunninghill and Warfield and a team from Windsor and Eton' in September 1812. It was won by eight wickets by Sunninghill. The Windsor team was probably the one usually called the Windsor and Eton Junior Cricket Club who played Sunninghill in September 1813 on Bachelors' Acre, where the result was declared a draw. This club regularly challenged teams from the locality, finishing the day with a dinner at the Swan Inn. Teams formed from the different regiments would play each other, or there would be matches between the military and civilians (August 1817).

In August 1826 at the Annual Bachelors' Revel on the Acre a cricket match formed part of the festivities, with fireworks in the evening, only marred by 'some boys wantonly throwing squibs among the company' – boys don't change! The following week there was a match in the Park between teams representing Berkshire and Surrey, which was won by Berkshire. To add to the occasion the King presented a 'noble buck' for the subsequent dinner. (HD)

Running Races

Any sport that could involve betting was popular and running races between two contestants were often reported. Heavy betting (December 1814) was laid on a race between Layton, a cabinet-maker, and Griffiths, a coachman, on a 6-mile course in the Great Park. Layton won by a hundred yards, picking up prize money of 5 guineas. He competed again (October 1816) but this time was beaten by ¾ mile by Wansall, a 'young man of Eton', in a time of just over 37 minutes (today a top runner would expect to complete the distance over a flat course in under half an hour). Prize money had gone up to 50 guineas for Wansall's match with a 'Kentish youth' (July 1817) which he won, but in a rematch in November he lost to the same challenger and with it a purse of 100 guineas.

Some running races were quirky. As reported on 21 January 1821 a blind pub landlord in London challenged a sighted man with eyes covered to a race across Waterloo Bridge: the blindfolded man was in the lead till he collided with a horse and cart 'which much damaged his head'! (HD)

Horse Racing at Ascot and Egham

Ascot Heath races, which had been inaugurated in 1711 during the reign of Queen Anne, were an important part of the social calendar. Forecasts and results of races were published in the *Express* in early June, and races were run over a four-mile course. Race week started then as it does today, the day after the Garter Ceremony in early June. The hotels and inns of the town and neighbourhood were busier than ever during race week, and coaches ran from the Swan Inn Windsor and the Christopher Inn Eton. Race-goers wanted entertaining in the evening, too, therefore the Theatre Royal was allowed to open during race weeks, always providing a varied programme. There were also balls and grand dinners in the evenings.

The first race week to be reported started on 15 June 1813. The major trophies were: His Majesty's Plate of 100 guineas, The Duke of York Plate of 50 guineas, The Gold Cup of 100 guineas (always on a Thursday) and the Billingbear Stakes of 100 guineas. The Duke of York had two horses in the race, and 'he had been particularly fortunate', winning two races (June 1813).

As today, Ascot races were attended by the rich and famous. Among the notables attending in June 1814 besides members of the Royal Family, were the Emperor of Russia, the King of Prussia, Marshal Blücher and Count Metternich, who were in England to celebrate Napoleon's defeat at Leipzig. During the Garter ceremony the day before the races the King of Prussia was invested as a Garter Knight. 1814 was also marked by the opening of a new stand, erected for the Duke of York, warden of Windsor Forest, next to that of the Queen and the Prince Regent.

Race week in June 1816 was said to be 'excessively wet', but the hotels and inns of Windsor were 'full beyond the extent of their accommodation'. The Queen with the royal princesses and the Duke of Gloucester attended on Tuesday, but the Prince Regent was detained in London. When he arrived on

Thursday, it was too wet for him to go to the races. The following year Ascot Heath was 'more fully attended than it had been for years, the weather too was favourable'.

A new royal stand from a design by 'Mr Nash' (presumably the architect John Nash 1752-1835) was completed at Ascot in May 1822. The King 'attended in the newly finished stand' on the first and third day. Mr Ramsbottom's four year old racehorse *Sir Huldibrand* won the Gold cup and the Forest Stakes of 50 guineas was won by the Duke of York's *Electress* (8 Jun 1822).

Egham races, held at Runnymede meadows since 1774, were equally popular. Race week was usually the last week in August, but could also be at other times during the summer and autumn. The first race week to be reported in the newspaper started on 25 August 1812 but it was marred by the scandal of a duel (see Duelling). The Gold Cup of Egham races, also worth 100 guineas, was won by *Sprightly* a four-year old colt owned by Mr Blake. *Sprightly* was sold for £500 guineas after the race. There were also the Magna Carta Stakes worth 50 guineas, won by the Duke of York with *Boaster*, and the Ladies' Plate, the Nobleman's and Gentleman's Plate and the Town Plate of £50 each.

There were balls in Egham Assembly Rooms but also in Windsor Town Hall during race week, and dinners in the great houses between Windsor and Egham. The theatre was usually open during the week, when it was in August, but in 1821 races started on 25 September. However, the theatre was opened under the patronage of the Duke of York. The Duke and Duchess of Clarence and Earl and Countess Harcourt attended racing that year (September 1821).

Race weeks were unfortunately marked by increased criminal activity. During Gold Cup day at Egham in 1814 the paper reported that 'The course was much infested with pickpockets'; a Windsor man had his gold snuff-box worth £60 stolen (August 1814). The Windsor magistrates sat every day during the week. Not only were there pickpockets, mainly from London, but gamblers, tricksters and prostitutes came to the races. In June 1814 the Mayor of Windsor banned all gaming tables in the borough during Ascot races. John Harrington was fined £5 at Windsor petty sessions for selling spirits at Ascot races without a licence (September 1813).

There were often accidents during race week. At Ascot in June 1813 one gentleman was 'rode over..., and his head very severely cut'. Two days later a chariot 'with some ladies inside and a gentleman on the dicky, was overturned'. The gentleman 'lies in a very dangerous state at Sunninghill Wells'. At Egham that year Mr Knowley, returning from a post-race dinner, overturned his chaise into a ditch. The chaise fell on top of him and 'he cannot possibly recover'. His horse had to be killed (August 1813). But the worst accident occurred in August 1828. The paper reported:

> One of Tolladay's eight-oared cutters was returning with a party of nineteen, consisting of men women and children, from Egham Races, a little beyond Datchet-bridge it struck on some stakes in the river, at a place where formerly an eel-weir existed.

The boat sank and 'melancholy to relate not less than nine of them perished', including three children. One man, however, was 'so insensible from intoxication, that he was not aware of the danger until he was rescued from the sinking boat'.

The last Egham races were held the following year, in August 1829. The paper stated that they were in future to be held on Ascot Heath, but also recorded that 'the extreme beauty of the weather had a palpable effect on the attendance, which was not only very numerous, but included many of the nobility of his Majesty's Court'. The King only attended on the Wednesday (August 1829). Racing at Runnymede seems to have been resumed by 1836, but the London gangs resumed their operations too and the course was closed for good in 1884.

Horticultural shows

In the early 19th century, horticultural shows in Windsor were not large events as we know them today, but small, select gatherings of gentlemen at one of the inns, showing just one variety of produce, while having a fine dinner with speeches.

The inns most often mentioned were the Star and Garter in Peascod Street, the Three Tuns near the Guildhall and especially the Hope Inn. This last public house was on Frogmore Road, the continuation of Park Street via Frogmore to Staines, which was later lost when the road was closed in about 1850.

Regular annual events included Cucumber shows in March, Pinks and Carnations in May, June and July, Gooseberries in July and Melons in August. In July 1827, the newspaper reported:

> A meeting of gardeners and gentlemen of the neighbourhood was held at the Hope Inn for the purpose of establishing a society to be called

'The Windsor Horticultural Society.' The society was formed, thirty-five gentlemen declared themselves members, and signed the resolutions. A committee and a secretary were appointed.

At the Cucumber Show in March 1828, six prizes were awarded for 'very superior fruit', all measuring 13 to 14 inches in length, though back in 1815 Royal gardeners had grown specimens of 4ft 10ins and 5ft 4ins, one of which was presented to Princess Charlotte. Across the river at Salt Hill, some cucumbers as long as seven feet were reported.

Exhibitors of pinks and carnations had to show 12 blooms of different sorts, and pay a substantial subscription. At the Carnation Show at the Star and Garter in July 1827 this was 10s 6d, with an extra 4 shillings for dinner and the First Prize was a handsome silver cup, value five guineas. At the same show, the subscription for gooseberries was five shillings each to show 12 berries, three of each of four colours.

The annual Melon Show or Melon Feast appears to have been quite a large event. It was reported at the beginning of August in every edition of the paper, and was well established before 1812. Prizes were awarded for flavour and appearance in different size categories, and prize-winners appear to have been growers from the Royal gardens or the large estates such as St Leonards. On one occasion at the Hope Inn, the first prize was awarded for a scarlet fresh melon,' perhaps one of the finest ever shown', both in regard to size, flavour and weight. The company all agreed that it was the best they had ever seen. After the prizes were given, they sat down to 'a most excellent dinner, and the day terminated with hilarity'. (SA)

Inns, Hotels and Taverns.

During the early nineteenth century, Windsor had a reputation for having more public houses than any other town in Berkshire. The presence of the two barracks and the movements of the Court swelled the local population and created a demand for different types of establishment. Pigot's 1830 Directory lists five inns and hotels, 30 taverns and public houses, and in addition there were many unlisted beerhouses.

Many are mentioned by name in the newspaper, some as meeting-places for grand dinners and celebrations and others, more notoriously, for events leading to the Magistrates' Court. It was customary at that time to hold Coroners' inquests in public houses and the paper has numerous such reports. Property auctions were commonly held in the town centre inns.

A traveller arriving from the north via Eton High Street and over Windsor Bridge would immediately pass the Crown and Anchor on the left, Swan Inn on the right, and the Royal Oak could be seen in Datchet Lane to the left. Further up Thames Street was the Adam and Eve near to the theatre on the right, with the Crispin across the road in the row of houses in the castle ditch. The Red Lion was on the corner of Bier Lane (now River Street) and finally, opposite the Castle, was the White Hart.

From the south, along Spital Road, was the Stag and Hounds and then closer to town the Merry Wives of Windsor and Jolly Gardeners. Peascod Street had many more, including the Sun, Bull, Crown and Star and Garter.

The road from Old Windsor and Staines at that time passed through Frogmore and Park Street. Along the road from Frogmore was the Hope Inn, and in Park Street the Two Brewers, Black Horse and New Inn. Others clustered round the Town Hall and Market Place opposite the Castle Inn included the Three Tuns, Ship and Horse and Groom on Castle Hill. Tucked away in George Street opposite the Castle was, amongst others, the Spread Eagle.

All were very different in character, depending on their location and clientele.

The grand dinners and celebrations, in addition to those held at the Town Hall, were at the Castle Inn, White Hart, Hope at Frogmore, Star and Garter and Swan. Royal birthdays and anniversaries were frequent opportunities for the gentry to gather for dinner, speeches, loyal toasts and entertainment by a military band. For example, there were annual dinners at the Swan in May, as reported in 1818 and 1819, for the Gentlemen of Windsor and Eton to celebrate the birthday of King George III, despite his incapacity, and a public dinner at the Hope Inn for Princess Augusta's birthday in October. Tickets were 4 shillings in 1822 and 5 shillings in 1823. As part of the Coronation celebrations for King George IV in 1821, there was a public dinner at the Castle Inn and on the first anniversary of his accession in February 1822 a 'large and respectable party' dined at the Star and Garter. The Bachelors of Windsor met regularly at the Swan in October to celebrate the anniversary of the erection of their obelisk on Bachelors' Acre in 1810. Charles Knight was treasurer of the Windsor Association for the Protection of Persons from Felons and Thieves which held its annual meeting at the Castle

Inn, followed by dinner. Members of the Windsor Horticultural Society dined regularly at the Hope Inn.

Civic occasions were also celebrated. In September 1819, following the election of George Davis as Mayor of Windsor and Edward Bovington as Justice of the Peace, a 'sumptuous' dinner was given at the Castle Inn by Corporation members Legh, Bedborough, Baverstock and Rendall. In June 1826, after Sir Richard Hussey Vivian was made a Freeman of the Royal Borough and proposed as MP, dinners were held at both the Castle Inn (hosted by Sir Richard) and White Hart (hosted by John Ramsbottom MP). The laying of the foundation stone of the new parish church in September 1820 was celebrated with a dinner at the Castle Inn, and the opening of Windsor Bridge in June 1824 called for a dinner at the Swan for the Mayor and Corporation. The Swan was also chosen in May 1826 to become a regular meeting place for the Masonic Lodge of St John No 359.

The common lodging houses of George Street were the most frequent scenes of drunken brawls and criminal behaviour, although the Crispin and Red Lion in Thames Street were also sometimes mentioned. In October 1829, the landlord of the Crispin was charged with allowing people to play cards on his premises! The Star and Garter, possibly because of its proximity to George Street via Goswell Lane, was targeted by thieves on many occasions. A haunch of mutton was stolen in January 1821 and traced to George Street, some forks and goblets were stolen in April 1826 and some potatoes in October 1827.

The Spread Eagle in George Street was commonly referred to as the Split Jack, and the Black Horse there was less reputable than the pub of the same name in Park Street.

In April 1829, after a drunken brawl at the Split Jack, three men were charged with riotous conduct after being abusive to the landlord and his customers. They were all committed to prison, in default of bail to keep the peace.

One notorious landlord, Haines, whose name was frequently in the newspaper for all the wrong reasons, was variously described as a vagabond and a one-eyed brothel-keeper. In September 1829 he was accused of assaulting a young woman for non-payment of rent, which she denied. When he claimed in his defence that she had hit him first, and said that his character was well-known in Windsor as he had lived here for 76 years, there was laughter. He was fined heavily.

The names of William Chell and Henry and Mary Wheeler were also well-known, and in August 1826 they were charged with keeping disorderly houses in George Street. Squabbles between the female residents of the Split Jack sometimes arose over rent payments, and in December 1829 Eliza Ball was assaulted by two other ladies.

> Eliza Ball stated that on Tuesday night last, about a quarter before nine o'clock, she was at the Black Horse public house when Nance Hillier and Stephena Winter came in, and because complainant had lately come to Windsor, began to abuse her and ask her to pay her footing. There were as many as ten present who were witnesses that she had paid it at the Spread Eagle, commonly called the Split Jack, in George Street. This however, the defendants would not believe, and said they would have it again or else have it out of her bones. She then went out of the house with the intention of going home, and the defendants followed her.

A fight and much bad language ensued because, as Hillier claimed, Eliza Ball felt herself above them, and they wished to make her know that she was no better than themselves. She was discharged, but Winter was fined 5 shillings and 14/6 costs, part of which she borrowed from her friend and the rest she paid from her purse (the corner of her handkerchief).

The same issue reported a fight between the landlord of the Two Brewers and three customers who, having consumed three pots of beer and three pipes of tobacco, appeared to be about to leave without paying.

Inquests were commonly carried out at the public house nearest to where a body was found, so the Crown and Anchor, Swan and Red Lion, being nearest to the river, would often be used in the case of a drowning. In July 1823, there was an inquest at the Swan Inn for 24-year-old Robert Anderson who drowned while bathing in the river, and in July 1824 there were two in the same week for young children who drowned, John Grant aged three and John Fish aged four. In September 1825 the Red Lion was the scene of the inquest into the death of Private Patrick Brown, drowned while swimming in the river with 50 other soldiers.

The Crown and Anchor, as well as receiving victims from the river, was also close to the wharves. In March 1828 George Toppin was crushed while lifting masses of stone from a barge to Mr Merryman's stonemason's yard and the verdict was 'Accident'.

One prolonged inquest which was extensively reported was at the Jolly Gardeners in Lower Peascod Street (now St Leonard's Road) in September 1825 on Thomas Cooper 24, who was shot while stealing fruit from an orchard. William Blowfield (otherwise known as Old Whackey) was a market gardener opposite the Cavalry Barracks and was plagued for four years with the theft of his best fruit. One Saturday, after midnight, he challenged three young men in his orchard, then fired off a shotgun towards them as they ran away. All three were injured, and Thomas Cooper died from his injuries. The inquest found that he had nearly 70 shotgun pellets, including six in his heart and several in his lungs. After an adjournment, the Coroner produced a new Act which had only become operative from 1 August. Before that act, Cooper and his companions could only have been committing trespass, and Blowfield would have been charged with murder, but afterwards they had committed a felony. Since Blowfield had called on them to surrender and they had run away, he was justified in firing at them and a verdict of justifiable homicide was recorded.

The Free House (later known as the Prince of Wales) in Clewer Lane (now Oxford Road) was the venue for an inquest in August 1829 on Thomas Russell, aged 82, whose body was found in 'a wretched hovel' close by. Although he had died a natural death, he seemed to have been greatly neglected 'as holes were actually eaten in his body by vermin.' The jury returned a verdict of 'Died by the visitation of God'.

Property sales and auctions were conducted at various inns around the town, and there are many examples, usually on the front page of the newspaper. In September 1813, the Crown and Anchor was auctioned at the White Hart Inn 'possessing many peculiar advantages, and numerous excellent accommodations, admirably situated near Windsor Bridge. It is most substantially built, in perfect repair, and commands a very extensive frontage'. At the Swan Inn in January 1813, a valuable lot was auctioned.

> Sundry extensive and desirable FREEHOLD PREMISES, admirably suited for business on the Banks of the Thames, at the extremity of BEER LANE and the GOSWELLS; comprising a cheerful, elevated and comfortable COTTAGE, with a large GARDEN, amply stocked and nearly inclosed by walls. A spacious and lofty BRICK BUILDING used as the DISSENTERS' MEETING-HOUSE; and THREE substantial HOUSES adjoining, all in good repair, and let to eligible yearly tenants, producing

a rental of £120 per annum, and commanding Five Borough and County Votes.

It is clear that the numerous public houses were busy and well-used for various purposes. Of those mentioned above, many have closed within living memory. The Three Tuns, Two Brewers, Royal Oak and Horse and Groom are examples of the few that remain. (SA)

Bachelors' Acre Revels and Celebrations

By 1812, Bachelors' Acre was well-established as the social centre of Windsor when it came to outdoor sports and pastimes.

In the mid 18th century, the Society of Bachelors of Windsor had been founded to safeguard the amenities. Not all members were unmarried, so it was an association made up of leading citizens of the day, rather like the modern Rotary Club.

By the end of that century, the Acre had been much neglected. It was used as a drain for the houses in the High Street, had been used for bull-baiting and was full of rubbish. As the Golden Jubilee of King George III approached, the Bachelors set about filling in the open sewers and restoring the amenities, and celebrated with an Ox Roast on 25 October 1809. This was attended, as part of a day-long programme of celebrations by Queen Charlotte, the Duke of York and other Royal Dukes and Princesses, although the King himself was not well enough to attend. The following May, the Bachelors erected an obelisk in the centre of the Acre, to record the Jubilee event, and held a cricket match, which would previously have been impossible. The obelisk has since been moved, and now stands at the eastern corner, near Victoria Street.

By the time of the launch of the *Windsor and Eton Express* in 1812, there was a regular programme of revels and celebrations, often to commemorate Royal birthdays. The Bachelors did themselves proud with regular dinners, for example in May 1813 they dined at the Crown Inn, Peascod Street, to celebrate the anniversary of the Obelisk, and in October of that year they dined at the Swan Inn in Thames Street to celebrate the anniversary of the jubilee, entertained by the band of the 55th Regiment. They announced forthcoming events in the newspaper, such as this one from 27 July 1817:

Part of a diorama made by Judith Ackland and Mary Stella
Edwards which is occasionaly on show at the Windsor & Royal
Borough Museum. It depicts the ox roast held in 1809 to
celebrate the beginning of the 60th year of the reign of George III.

The Bachelors of Windsor intend having a REVEL in their Acre to celebrate the birthday of HRH Prince Regent on 12 August. Back-swording, running in sacks, and a variety of other amusements.

(Back-swording was a traditional country martial art, using wooden swords with leather handles).

There were Easter Fairs in April and Horse, Cow, Cattle and Sheep Fairs in October, together with stalls and booths in the High Street.

The largest Revel was held in August each year to celebrate the birthday of the Prince Regent, later King George IV, and his coronation was celebrated in July 1821 with an ox roast on the Acre and dinners at the Town Hall and the Castle Inn.

Travelling circuses and menageries were popular, sometimes in quick succession. In November 1828, the newspaper reported that the pleasure fair was generally considered to have been the largest and best that had been held for 'these fourteen years past.' As well as all the stalls, there were the rival menageries of Atkins and Wombwell on the Acre, with side-shows, giants, dwarfs and pig-faced ladies!

The quantities of food and drink consumed during ox roasts and other Revels were huge. The newspaper reported the 1821 coronation festivities as follows:

> On Wednesday evening, the gentlemen of the Committee assembled in the Town Hall, and thence proceeded to the bottom of Peascod street, where a Procession was formed, consisting of a miscellaneous band – the Charity children with staves and favours – the Committee wearing purple favours and some bearing flags – the Ox intended to be roasted, whole, trussed and spitted and placed on a wain drawn by four beautiful horses – four sheep on a second carriage – and another Ox on a third. Each of the waggons was attended by a party of butchers, whose concert of marrow-bones and cleavers was more distinguished for its force than its harmony. The procession went forward up Peascod street, down Thames street to the Bridge, returned through High street and Park street, and finally delivered its old English fare to the Bachelors' Acre. The cheers of the multitude throughout were loud and general.

The fires were lighted at 9 o'clock, and about 12 the ox was put down. 'A finer animal was never seen, it weighing 94 stone, and being particularly fat.' In addition, there were 100 stone of roast and boiled beef, 5000 small loaves, 2000 coronation cakes and 24 barrels of beer. The holiday atmosphere was enhanced by the ringing of bells; flags were flying from the Castle and 'the unfinished tower of the new Parish Church'. Crowds were drawn to the Acre where the ox was roasting. 'Near the side of the fire on which the ox was roasting was a platform raised, sufficiently large for the animal to be cut up on, and to be distributed with bread and beer. On a similar platform was a stage for cutting up the sheep'. At 2 o'clock a small cannon gave a signal for 'the commencement of the distribution' of meat, bread, coronation cakes and beer.

The report concluded that there were happy groups of families and friends, and although many displayed symptoms of the potency of the ale, there were no disturbances of the general harmony.

Two years later, in celebration of the King's arrival in Windsor, the feast included 350 stone of beef, mutton and veal, 50 stone of hams, 2400 loaves, 1200 pounds of plum puddings, 2000 lettuces and 1000 heads of celery. This was washed down with two glasses of wine per person in addition to eighteen barrels of ale and one butt of porter.

Children were always well catered-for on these and other occasions, including those from the poorest areas. The newspaper reported on 25 October 1828:

> On Monday forenoon, the children of the National Schools of Windsor and the neighbourhood were regaled by our worthy Mayor, ROBERT TEBBOTT esq with a feast of buns and ale in the Batchelors' Acre. The number of children present was upwards of 350, and a gayer, a merrier, or a more delighted group, it would have been difficult to conceive or collect. Several of the ladies and gentlemen of Windsor and Eton were present to witness the felicity, and after drinking the following toasts "with appropriate honours" – viz – "The King – God bless him!" with four cheers, and "The Mayor" with three.

Inevitably, not all of the Revels passed off without incident. In August 1826, the marching bands and fireworks were spoiled by boys throwing squibs, and in August 1828 a drunken brawl between soldiers and civilians spilled over to the High Street and The White Hart. Several soldiers were hurt, and five men were accused of Riot.

The presence of menageries with wild animals presented its own hazards, and a report of November 1828 said that as Wombwell's wild beast vans were proceeding along the bottom of Peascod Street, one of the men, named Stephen Stacey, being somewhat intoxicated, fell between the shafts, and was dreadfully trampled on and bruised by the horses. He was taken to The Merry Wives of Windsor for medical assistance, and it transpired that he was one of the men who had been badly mauled by a leopard a few weeks earlier.

The Revels followed a similar pattern every year. The bells of the Castle and Parish Church rang throughout the day. A Royal salute was fired at 9 am, followed by games until 1 o'clock. The Bachelors then marched around the Acre, displaying their colours, accompanied by a band, then adjourned to dinner. Further sports and contests of strength and skill followed in the afternoon until 8.30 pm, when there was a grand firework display. All levels of society took part, from Royalty and Aristocracy to apprentices, labourers, farmers, soldiers and tradesmen. At the end of the evening, 'the Bachelors and their friends betook themselves to their tent in the Acre, and caroused with most happy hearts till past midnight.'

The newspaper concluded:

As the Bachelors Revel is one among few of our national and popular amusements which has been left behind by the rapid March of Intellect, or escaped annihilation by that 'stern rugged nurse' of national morality, the police, we feel some little interest in its existence, and hope and trust that the Bachelors Revel will continue to be kept up with spirit and energy equal to that displayed on the present occasion.

The Revels did continue until 1855, with a variety of sports and competitions, and an ox roast was held as recently as 2002 on the occasion of the Queen's Golden Jubilee and in 2012 for the Diamond Jubilee. (SA)

The Guildhall

In 1812 the Guildhall or Town Hall stood as it was designed by Thomas Fitch and completed in 1690 to replace the old Market House. It was 'appointed the Guildhall' during a council meeting on 17 October 1690 and consisted of the Corn Market enclosed by pillars on all four sides (but none in the centre) with a large chamber above and vaulted cellars below. The cellars were rented out to local tradesmen. The chamber was divided into three, a large Hall and two smaller rooms as Council Chamber and Jury Room. A covered staircase led up to the Hall at the back of the building. Many royal portraits were displayed on the walls. In February 1823 George IV presented a large portrait of himself to the Guildhall collection, painted by Sir Thomas Lawrence.

The newspaper referred to the building as the Guildhall or Town Hall, often in the same paragraph. The Hall was in regular use not only as a Guildhall with council and public meetings as well as Magistrates and Coroners Courts, but also as a Town Hall with public entertainment, celebrations, balls and dinners. The new Mayor of Windsor was sworn into office at the Guildhall each year; the first one in this period was John Snowden in October 1812. He dined with 'the most respectable gentlemen of the town and neighbourhood' including officers of the 29th Regiment at the Town Hall. There were many other public dinners in the Hall, in October 1822, 'Upwards of a hundred and twenty sat down to turtle, venison and every delicacy the season afforded'.

The first ball of the period in November 1812 'was numerously and fashionably attended. The dancing was kept up with great spirit until a very late hour'. In January 1815 three balls were announced in the newspaper for the birthdays of the King, the Queen and the Duke of Cambridge all within a few weeks; ladies paid 7s and gentlemen 14s. Balls were regularly held in this largest hall in Windsor, not just to celebrate Royal occasions, but there were regular subscription balls, and dances each year at Christmas and Easter, or to celebrate military victories, or the departure of a regiment. However, it is difficult to believe that 120 people fitted comfortably into this space. In November 1827 a ball 'in honour of Princess Augusta's birthday, boasted of a very large assemblage of the nobility and gentry of the town and neighbourhood, amounting to upwards of 120', including officers of the 2nd Life Guards and 21st Fusiliers. 'The display of beauty and fashion was most brilliant'. Refreshments were always available at these occasions.

Then there were the concerts and lectures; admission charges for a vocal and instrumental concert in May 1815 were 3s and 5s 6d; and at a lecture on French literature in April 1821 the band of the Royal Horse Guards provided entertainment. Mr Bird used his 'Grand Transparent Orrery and a balloon' to illustrate a lecture on astronomy in September 1825, which was very popular; he had given his lectures before at the Theatre Royal and the Swan Inn.

BY PERMISSION OF THE WORSHIPFUL THE MAYOR.

GRAND CONCERT.

MR. C. QUARTERMAN (from the Royal Academy of Music) most respectfully informs the Nobility, Gentry, Inhabitants of Windsor, Eton, and their Vicinities, that there will be a Grand Concert of Vocal and Instrumental Music at the TOWN HALL, WINDSOR, on WEDNESDAY, OCT. 22, 1828, by permission of the Right Hon. the Directors of the Royal Academy of Music. The performance will be entirely by the pupils of that Institution (with the exception of Mr. Sapio.)

Leader, Mr. Seymour—*Conductor,* Mr. Quarterman.

Solo Performers :—Pianoforte, Mr. Quarterman ; Violin, Mr. Mawkes and Mr. Blagrove ; Horn, Mr. Daniell ; principal Violincello, Mr. Lucas ; principal Hautboy, Mr. Cooke ; Double Bass, Mr. Howell.

Principal Vocal Performers :—Miss Bellchamber, Miss Duff, Mr. Sapio (from the Theatre Royal Covent Garden), Mr. A. Sapio, Mr. F. Smith.

Tickets, 5s. each, to be had at Mr. J. B. Brown, bookseller, Castle-street, Windsor ; Messrs. Wetton's, Egham, Maidenhead, and Chertsey.

Further particulars will be duly announced.

The Windsor Quarter Sessions were always held at the Guildhall, with the Mayor as one of the Magistrates. But also the occasional inquest was heard there; in June 1824 an inquest was held on the body of a four-year-old boy who had drowned in a pond in the Goswells.

Finally there were the meetings of various societies or groups. The Wesleyan missionary society and the Bible Society celebrated their anniversaries in December 1823 and in July 1824. Annual General Meetings of the Dispensary, the Savings Bank, the National School etc took place in the Guildhall. In October 1827 the shareholders of the Windsor Royal Gas Light Company met to discuss the intricacies of lighting Windsor by gas, and whether to use coal gas or that produced by oil or resin.

In 1828 the council proposed to extend and renovate the Guildhall and to confine the butcher's shambles at the back of the building to one area within the extension (this is the site of the present museum). Houses behind the Guildhall were bought up and demolished, Mr Bedborough's plan was accepted and the foundation stone was laid by Alderman James Eglestone on 27 June 1829. The extension was completed in May 1830 and opened without any ceremony, possibly because of the ill health of George IV.

Watercolour of the Guildhall painted in the late 1700s by Samuel Evans, who was an art master at Eton College. It shows the building as both Charles Knights would have known it.

The River

Windsor Bridge

A bridge across the River Thames has existed at Windsor since c.1170. In 1242 a new one was constructed of oak trees felled from the Forest of Windsor. The bridge was repaired at frequent intervals over the centuries. By the beginning of the nineteenth century it was in such a dilapidated condition that it was decided to construct a more sturdy bridge.

Windsor Bridge in 1820

Courtesy of the Royal Windsor Website

To build the new bridge at Windsor, as with any major repairs, required an Act of Parliament. In August 1818 an advertisement in the *Windsor Express* reported that a Bill was to be presented to Parliament for the 'rebuilding, widening and enlarging' of the present timber bridge over the River Thames at Windsor. The works included removing some buildings to make a new approach way and also to increase the tolls for crossing the bridge and going underneath it by boat or barge. In September that year a notice was put in the paper by the Town Clerk John Secker, asking to receive plans and specifications for the new bridge from interested parties.

In May 1819 the act for the construction of the bridge was presented to the House of Commons by Windsor MP John Ramsbottom and was later ratified by the House of Lords in 1820.

Charles Hollis was chosen as the architect. His plans for a cast iron bridge were exhibited at the Guildhall in 1821. Interested builders were asked to submit their tenders. Cast iron was a material, which Hollis had used previously in the rebuilding of Windsor Parish Church. Local builder William Moore was selected by the Corporation and promised to have the bridge finished by the end of November 1822.

In March 1822 the old bridge was taken down and the materials were sold for £100. Whilst it was dismantled an iron footbridge was constructed to allow the crossing between Windsor and Eton on foot, and a temporary ferry service started to operate.

On 10 July 1822 the cornerstone of the new bridge was laid with a Masonic ceremony led by the Duke of York who represented the Duke of Sussex, Grandmaster of the United Grand Lodge of England, together with other Grand Lodge officers. The *Windsor Express* of 13 July 1822 chronicles the event in detail: 'Every window in the line of the procession was occupied by elegantly dressed ladies', eager to witness this event and the chance of spotting the Duke of York. The procession consisted of some 300 masons in full regalia intermixed with a number of prominent Windsorians. There was extremely limited accommodation to view the actual ceremony and a wooden platform was erected for the use of the Masons in the procession.

During the ceremony the Duke of York placed a cup with a number of coins, a coronation Medal of 1822 and a silver plate into the cornerstone itself. The plate was inscribed with the names of all those attending, including Charles Knight and the two MPs of the Borough John Ramsbottom and Major General Sir Herbert Taylor.

Charles Hollis then presented the plans of the bridge and William Moore the builder presented a silver trowel to the Duke of York. He consecrated the stone with the corn, oil and wine. The Duke of York was later introduced to the Mayor, architect and the builder and was presented with the silver trowel used in the laying of the stone. The trowel was afterwards returned by the Duke to the Corporation of Windsor and is now in the museum. A dinner for 200 guests was held at the Guildhall.

During the excavation for the new foundations for the bridge piers some interesting archaeological finds were unearthed, including a number of horse shoes of some antiquity and of curious shape, a seventeenth century spur, and several coins including a gold quarter noble of Edward III.

The final bridge pier was difficult to construct as no firm ground could be reached due to the volume of water. This was overcome, however, by using the army to help. In August 1822 40 to 60 members of the 7th Royal Fusiliers used four chain pumps to pump out the water for a number of days and were relieved by new soldiers every four hours.

The construction of the bridge was not without disaster as an account in the *Windsor Express* of 25 May 1822 describes: James Stebbs, a labourer working on one of the piers within a coffer dam slightly lost his balance and grabbed the pier to secure himself, by doing this he dislodged part of the bridge machinery and part of the pile driver mechanism known as a 'monkey' fell and smashed into his right hand. He had to have three fingers amputated and was sadly unable to go back to work for quite some while.

Later that year a barge called the *Prince Regent,* owned by a Mr Gibson of Marlow carrying paper and flour, crashed into an island known as the *Cobler* trying to negotiate the bridgeworks, and finally grounded on the Windsor shore. It 'received great damage'.

The completion of the bridge was marred by the death of its builder, William Moore, in October 1823. The work was continued by his executor, a Mr Baldock.

Due to circumstances beyond the builder's control the bridge did not open until the 1 June 1824. It cost £15,000. Under the terms of the Act allowing the rebuilding, tolls were imposed on horses and carriages (apart from those used by the Royal family and the army) though foot passengers were allowed across for free.

The ceremony for the opening of the bridge on 1 June 1824, unlike the Masonic stone laying, was a very quiet affair. The Mayor was accompanied by the Borough Chaplain and the MP for Windsor, the architect Charles Hollis and the son of William Moore, together with other people who had been involved in the building of the bridge. The toll gate was closed and the architect presented the Mayor with a silver key. The Town Clerk read a

The New Windsor Bridge in 1830. Picture from the Royal Windsor Website

proclamation declaring the bridge open, three cheers were given and the procession returned to the Swan Inn as a cannon was fired from the town wharf. In the evening a dinner was held at the Swan Inn - assembled diners were entertained by comedians and singers and ended with toasts wishing 'prosperity to the Town of Windsor'. (EK)

River Tragedies

Just as at the top of the town the Castle dominated life, so below it did the River Thames, acting as a vital artery for the transport of goods, and a source of water. It was also used for recreational purposes: for fishing, boating, skating when it was frozen in winter and swimming in summer. But water is a treacherous element and tragic stories of drownings appear frequently in the paper, often of young people.

In January 1814 a thirteen-year-old servant girl, Karia Skinner, drowned when she was sent from the house where she worked in Eton to fetch a kettle of water when the pump failed. It was believed that her foot had slipped on the bank while reaching down and that she tumbled over. Thirteen-year-old Eton boys seem to have been vulnerable: one drowned while out rowing (1 April 1821), another when harmlessly floating paper boats with his friends in a stream: he climbed up the bank to see better but slipped and was carried away to his death (14 December 1822). In June 1826, 13-year-old Ralph Deane, who couldn't swim, went into the water with a friend; they were new to the school and perhaps didn't know that there was a prohibition on swimming at the spot they chose. Ralph drowned; his friend survived.

ONE GUINEA REWARD.

WHEREAS a LITTLE BOY, in Petticoats, four years old, was unfortunately DROWNED, on Friday Evening last, off the Kempshot, in Bier-lane, Windsor, the body of which has not yet been found,—

Notice is hereby given, that the above Reward will be paid to any person who shall recover the same, and give notice to his disconsolate Parents, WM. and M. FISH, Windsor.

June 26, 1824.

During a single week in June 1824 two very young boys drowned, one aged three, one four, at a time when the river was running high after heavy rain. An inquest was held on the three-year-old, John Grant, son of a shoe-maker, who had been playing with a friend at Black Potts on the Eton bank when he fell in. A man stripped and jumped in but, unable to reach the child, he took a boat. He got within twenty yards of the boy when the child sank; the body was later recovered from under Datchet Bridge. (The bridge no longer exists.) The other little boy, 'still in petticoats' (that is not yet wearing trousers), came from Bier Lane. His parents advertised a reward of a guinea for anyone who could recover their son's body. In another sad case the five-year-old son of 'a poor man named Copas' drowned while trying with other children to cross Clewer Mill stream to get turnips from a field.

Soldiers could get into difficulties while bathing, often because they could not swim. In May 1827 an inquest was held on the body of Private Patrick Brown of the 21st Royal Fusiliers who drowned at Clewer, even though there were more than 50 other soldiers bathing at the time. On a Saturday evening in the following summer Anthony Moore, a corporal of the Grenadier Guards and a man 'of an exemplary character' had, despite being unable to swim, gone into the river about a mile above the bridge. He was swiftly carried away by the current and 'almost immediately sank'. Onlookers stood helplessly by until an Eton boy in a skiff, Lord Hillsborough, rowed to the body and lifted it to the surface with an oar:

> Further assistance was immediately procured; and the unfortunate man, having been landed, was conveyed to the Swan Inn, Clewer, one of his comrades, with praiseworthy promptitude, stripping off his garments, and laying them on the body, to preserve, if possible, the vital spark (5 July 1828).

He did show signs of life so was taken to the Infantry Hospital, but in the end died.

There were successful rescues. In November 1821 seven men were returning from work at the Mustard Mill in Staines, one of them a new worker who had been treating his new acquaintances with beer,

> which rendered them more wanton than prudent; for though the part they had occasion to go over was not more than leg-deep, they by some playfulness got into the Mill-stream, where the rapidity of the current upset the boat and precipitated the seven men into a depth of ten feet.

That only four of them drowned was owing to the courage of a former sailor who 'evinced the true spirit of a British tar': he tied a rope round his middle and dived in, managing to bring up three of the seven, who 'under Divine Providence' were 'restored to their families and friends'. There were desperate scenes on the water's edge as word got around, and the wife of one of the dead was with difficulty prevented from throwing herself in too. The four who drowned were buried in Staines churchyard. But that was not the end of distress for the families for, as the paper reported a week later, the story came to the notice of 'resurrection' men (those who dug up bodies to sell for doctors' dissections), and three of the bodies were taken from the their graves by resurrectionists.

In 1823 two young men were rewarded with £1 each for rescuing a woman who threw herself into the river (5 July). She was saved, but suicides were not infrequent. Often the victims were young women betrayed in love, drowning themselves in despair. This was was probably true of an 18-year-old, Julia Horn, whose body was pulled from the river in April 1828. At the inquest her sister, with whom she had been lodging, said that she had been supposed that day to go by coach to London and take up a situation there, but had left shortly after 5am by the back door and was not seen again. The sister also revealed that, although Julia denied it, she believed that the girl was 'in the family way'.

But the saddest stories of bodies recovered were those of new-born babies, such as was reported in March 1823 when a 'newly-born male infant' was found in the Thames just below Windsor bridge. The body had been carefully 'wrapped in linen and old carpeting, secured with skewers'. The desparation of such mothers can be imagined, but if they were identified it was a capital offence. A distressing case reported in March 1816 was that of Sarah Cook of Aston in Oxfordshire, further up the Thames. She was married but the couple were no longer living together – whether the baby she carried was his or another man's was not revealed. In August of the previous year she had left her home, apparently for London, but at Ware she gave birth to a male child and then, only the next day, returned to Aston. That afternoon a 'country lad' walking along the river bank discovered the body of a baby boy at the water's edge, half-hidden under 'weeds'. Sarah was immediately apprehended and at first denied guilt: her baby had been a girl which, she said, had died at birth at a relative's house in Hertford. Her story was soon disproved and she confessed, expressing 'sorrow for what she had done'.

When brought to trial six months later she was found guilty and the judge passed sentence: she was to be hanged and then her body given for dissection. The paper reported that:

During the whole trial she appeared quite callous and insensible of her awful situation; but the Learned Judge himself was so much affected at passing the sentence, that he was more than once interrupted by his tears.

Whatever his tears there was no recommendation for mercy and three days later the brutal sentence was carried out.

Suicides and drownings still occur, and women may abort or abandon unwanted babies, but at least there are no more pathetic little bundles in the river. (HD)

Mayors of Windsor 1811-1830

George III

1811	Edward Parker	
1812	John Snowden	(Son was a Grocer)
1813	William Hanson	Silversmith
1814	John Hatch	
1815	James Atkins	(Son was an ironmonger)
1816	Charles Layton	Confectioner
1817	Charles Knight	Bookseller and Printer
1818	Edward Bovingdon	(Son was a brewer)
1819	George Davis	Locksmith and Smoke-jack maker

George IV

1820	John Banister	Butcher
1821	James Egleston	Hatter
1822	John Chapman	Surgeon
1823	Charles Layton	Confectioner
1824	Edward Brown	
1825	John Clode	Inn Keeper (Castle Hotel)
1826	John Voules	Coal Merchant
1827	Thomas Jenner	Builder
1828	Robert Tebbot	Builder
1829	James Church	Chemist

William IV

1830	John Banister	Butcher

Personalities

Top: George Davis and James Bedborough

(Royal Borough of Windsor & Maidenhead Civic Collection)

Bottom: The Urn on the Ramsbottom memorial in Old Windsor Churchyard (photo Pamela Marson)

The Right Honourable William Harcourt

(National Portrait Gallery)

Lord William Harcourt (1743-1830)

William Harcourt was born in 1742 and had a distinguished career in the army. He purchased the St Leonard's Hill Estate in 1782 and in 1787 he was made Deputy Ranger of Windsor Great Park by George III. After the death of his brother, George Simon Harcourt, second Earl Harcourt in 1809, William succeeded to his titles and estates. He also inherited the appointment of Master of the Horse to Queen Charlotte, which he held until her death in 1818. The *Windsor Express* later reported the sale of 10 of her carriage horses for £4,544 and 18 carriages for £1,077.

Lord Harcourt first appears in the *Windsor Express* in August 1812 where it was reported that he 'gave a splendid ball to nobility and gentry at St Leonard's Hill'. Although no members of the Royal family were present most of the distinguished nobility were there.

During a visit of the Duchess of Oldenburgh, Lord and Lady Harcourt accompanied the Royal family on a visit from Frogmore to Sandhurst and Eton College in May 1814. Members of the Royal family included Princesses Elizabeth and Mary, and the Duke of Sussex, complete with their respective retinues. After the visit to Eton College the Royal carriages proceeded to St Leonard's Hill for luncheon. The Royal party also stayed on for dinner. The *Express* said that: the Noble Lord entertained his illustrious visitors with a dinner, which for magnificence and taste has seldom been more surpassed (May 1814).

In August 1818 they attended a fete at Princess Elizabeth's Cottage (now the site of the Friary, Old Windsor). The event was attended by the Prince Regent. The *Express* describes the ladies being 'attired in a romantic simplicity as peasant girls and the gentlemen principally wearing the costume of rural life'. There was dancing in the ballroom which led to a large tent containing the supper room with a magnificent chandelier.

In 1820 Lord and Lady Harcourt reached their social pinnacle in society and entertained King George IV. The *Express* reports that 'his Majesty honoured the Earl and Countess Harcourt with his company to dinner at St Leonards'. This is the only time that the King is reported to have dined there. In 1828 the Harcourts celebrated their fiftieth wedding anniversary at St Leonard's Hill. Over 60 guests were invited who danced the night away.

As well as being socialites they were great benefactors to the poor and under- privileged of Windsor. Lady Harcourt had established a school in Clewer Green in 1806, known as the Harcourt School. In September1815 a deed was drawn up to ensure the continuance of the school and that income was guaranteed.

In 1815 William was involved with the formation of the Windsor General Dispensary, and when it opened in March 1818 he became its President.

His name appeared on most subscription lists published in the *Express*. In 1816 he contributed 10 guineas to provide food and fuel at a reduced cost to the poor, and in 1820 he gave £20 to help the poor 'during the present inclement weather'.

Lord William Harcourt died on 17 June 1830, aged 87, at his home at St Leonards Hill. Since he had no children his title became extinct. (EK)

George Davis (1760-1833)

The family of George Davis had been clock makers to the King for generations and he was apprenticed to his father John Davis (the third of that name) and became a locksmith and smoke jack* maker. He held a Royal Warrant as a locksmith and ironmonger to both George III and George IV, and designed some locks that were used by government offices. In 1819 he became Mayor of Windsor.

Because Davis was a great favourite of George III, his son George IV wanted to reward him and in 1820 offered him a knighthood. He refused the personal honour. Instead he asked if there could be something to pass down to all future Mayors of Windsor, to honour the town. George IV arranged for a medallion on a gold chain to be made and it was presented to Davis by John Ramsbottom MP. This was the first time that a mayoral chain had been presented by the monarch as they were usually given by the trade guilds of the town or city.

On the front of the medallion is the arms of the Corporation surmounted with the Royal Crown. The newspaper reported that the inscription on the reverse reads 'George Davis, Mayor, presented by his most sacred Majesty King George the Fourth 1820'. However do not believe everything you read in the papers because the actual inscription is: Presented by His Most Sacred Majesty King George the Fourth to the Mayor and Corporation of New Windsor MDCCCXX.

In 1830 the crown was removed and replaced above an extra gold embellishment added by William IV. On the reverse of this is inscribed: Enlarged and Ornamented by His Most Gracious Majesty King William the Fourth 1830

This has been passed down as George wished and is still worn by the Mayor of the Royal Borough of Windsor & Maidenhead at Windsor functions. A portrait of Davis wearing his chain is in the Mayor's Parlour in the Guildhall.

At a Court of Common Council held on Friday last, George Davis, Esq. Mayor, was invested, by command of his present Majesty, with a Gold Badge and Chain, as an insignia of office, to be worn by the Mayor for the time being, and his successors. The investiture was to have been performed by General Sir Herbert Taylor, one of the representatives of this Borough; but this gentleman, from various circumstances, was prevented from attending. Sir Herbert Taylor therefore requested John Ramsbottom, Esq., the other member for the Borough, to act as his substitute.

On the Medallion, which is pendant from the chain, are the Arms of the Corporation, surmounted with the Royal Crown; on the reverse is inscribed, "George Davis, Mayor, presented by his most sacred Majesty King George the Fourth, 1820."

The distinction thus conferred upon the Corporation of Windsor, by the favour of his present Majesty, is without any precedent in the municipal honours of the kingdom. The chains of the Lord Mayors of London and York, are the gifts of the several companies composing those Corporations. This most gracious grant of the King may be considered as an expression of his Majesty's esteem for a Borough, so long the favoured residence of his august father and family; and so associated in our history with some of the most glorious and estimable of England's monarchs.

We cannot avoid mentioning that the suggestion of this distinguished favour to the Corporation arose out of the personal disinterestedness of our present worthy Chief-magistrate. Mr. Davis, who was much esteemed by the late King, was on a recent occasion offered by his present Majesty the honour of knighthood. He declined the individual distinction; but expressed a desire that his Majesty's gracious intentions towards himself should merge in some expression of good opinion towards the Corporation, of which he (the Mayor) was the head. The King immediately gave orders at the Herald's College for the investment of the Mayor of Windsor with a gold chain; and we believe the order accompanied the grant of a similar honour to Sir Thomas Lawrence, as President of the Royal Academy.

108

The report of this enduring event in the newspaper is just a few paragraphs squeezed between two other unrelated news items. (PM)

*A smoke jack was a roasting spit with vanes placed inside the chimney which were turned by the hot air and this helped the smoke go up the chimney.

James Thomas Bedborough (1787–1860)

James Thomas Bedborough was born into a family who had been stonemasons for the past three generations. In 1804 he began a four year apprenticeship as a stonemason to his father, Thomas. He was promoted to King's Master Mason and worked at repairing Windsor Castle. One of his first major works was the construction of the Royal vaults beneath St George's Chapel, in 1812.

In September 1819 Bedborough was elected to the Windsor Corporation. He progressed through the hierarchy of the Council and became 'Chamberlain to the Poor' in 1823-4 and eventually became Mayor of Windsor in both 1846 and 1854.

In 1824 architect Jeffry Wyatt began a major rebuilding programme at Windsor Castle. Bedborough was selected as principal building contractor. He was particularly responsible for heightening the Round Tower. Bedborough worked at the Castle until the completion of the rebuilding in 1836. As well as working on the restoration he and his partner Robert Tebbott built the new Parish Church, which was completed in 1822.

Bedborough was paid handsomely for his building work at the Castle and with the proceeds was able to embark on his first property development in 1828. He built housing both for the wealthy and for the working classes. This included Clarence Crescent, where he built 12 fine villas laid out around a communal garden. In stark contrast with Clarence Crescent, Bedborough also built a double row of artisans' houses, known as South Place, which very quickly became slum dwellings. During the building the *Express* reported that five women 'of the lowest description were apprehended in one of Mr Bedborough's unfinished houses where they sheltered' and were sleeping rough (8 March 1828). In 1842 he created a new estate of villas at Upton Park in Slough.

In 1829 Bedborough enlarged the Guildhall for Windsor Corporation. He added a new brick extension to the existing building, effectively doubling the size of the Guildhall. This was his last work to be executed in central Windsor. He later moved into one of his villas in Clarence Crescent and died in Windsor in February 1860. (EK)

John Ramsbottom (c.1777-1845)

John Ramsbottom was born in London and educated at Eton College. He then had a brief spell in the army and on reaching his retirement he obtained the rank of Major and Commandant of the Clewer Volunteers.

In 1796 he went into partnership with William Legh and took over the running of the Windsor Bank and Brewery in Thames Street. These had been run previously by his uncle Richard Ramsbottom (c.1749 - 1813) and his father John (1745 - 1826), who had purchased the brewery in 1780 from Henry Isherwood.

The newspaper of 1814 records that £5348. 0s 2d was taken from the Hertford Coach, and a significant amount belonged to Ramsbottom's Bank. The perpetrator was later caught with money in his possession. In 1815 it was thought that the bank was about to collapse but this was only a temporary situation and it was later to reissue banknotes. In 1837 the bank and brewery were sold to Neville Reid and Company.

Henry Isherwood and his uncle Richard had both been Members of Parliament for Windsor and John Ramsbotton Jr followed in their footsteps and became the third 'Brewer' MP. His subsequent re-election is recorded in the *Windsor Express* of October 1812. In January 1819 he presented a Bill to Parliament to rebuild Windsor Bridge, which was ratified by the House of Lords in 1820. He remained an MP until his death.

He was also a prominent Freemason and in September 1820 he laid the foundation stone of the new parish church on behalf of the Duke of York and officiated at a similar ceremony for the foundation stone of the Windsor Bridge in July 1822.

Ramsbottom was a great donor to charity and is found on many of the subscription lists for good causes; in particular he gave the sum of 500 guineas for the rebuilding of the Parish Church. His bank also acted as treasurers for many local charities such as the Institution for Assisting Labouring Classes of Windsor and Clewer and for the subscription to the National School in 1820.

John Ramsbottom had two residences in the Windsor area – Clewer Lodge and Woodside in Old Windsor. He died at The Albany, London on 8 October 1845 and was buried at Old Windsor. (EK)

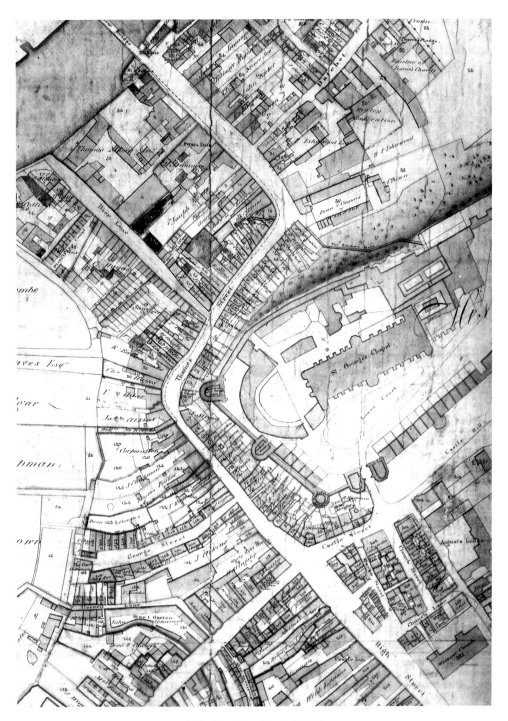

Windsor in about 1810

*King George III
in Old Age*

by Joseph Lee

*Supplied by Royal
Collection Trust /
© HM Queen
Elizabeth II 2012*

*Queen Charlotte
by John Hopkins*

*Supplied by Royal Collection Trust /
© HM Queen Elizabeth II 2012*

Princess Augusta
After Sir William Beechy

Princess Sophia
By Sir William Beechy

Princess Elizabeth
By Sir William Beechy

Princess Charlotte of Wales
By Denis Brownell Murphy

All four pictures
Supplied by Royal Collection Trust / © HM Queen Elizabeth II 2012

George IV wearing the Robes of State by Sir Thomas Lawrence.
This is a copy of the portrait in the Vatican Picture Gallery and was presented to
Windsor Corporation by the King in 1823. It hangs in the Guildhall at Windsor.
© Royal Borough of Windsor & Maidenhead Civic Collection.

Victoria , Duchess of Kent (1786-1861)
with Princess Victoria (1819-1901)

Supplied by Royal Collection Trust / © HM Queen Elizabeth II 2012

The Funeral Procession of the Princess Charlotte at Windsor

The town gate looking westwards down Castle Hill c.1765 by Paul Sandby
Supplied by Royal Collection Trust / © HM Queen Elizabeth II 2012

The Taglioni Windsor Coach
Painted by J. Pollard Engraved by RG Reeve

The Staffordshire Militia 1804
Courtesy of the National Army Museum

Royal Hunt
The Royal Collection © Her Majesty Queen Elizabeth II

Wellington at Waterloo

Engraving of Charles Knight Jr. by London Stereo Co. from a photograph. Published in The Family Friend *September 1875 to celebrate the presentation of the bust by Joseph Durham to Windsor Corporation on 14th June 1875*

A cartoon of the Camelopard
See page 58

The Cow Pock, early 1800s by H. Humphrey

The Duke of Wellington's duel with the Earl of Winchilsea at Battersea fields – 19th century print in the foyer of Wellington Hall.

© *King's College London Archives*

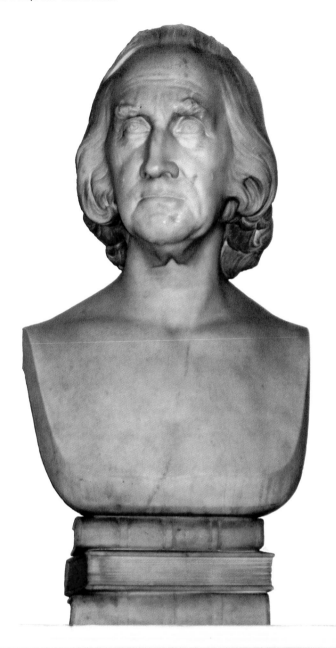

The bust of Charles Knight Jr. presented to Windsor Corporation on 14th June 1875. There is a similar one in the National Portrait Gallery. The sculptor was Joseph Durham.

Schools and Churches

Schools

There was a strong movement towards educating the disadvantaged poor by the time the Windsor newspaper appeared, a topic close to Charles Knight's heart. In December 1819 he wrote:

> Education of the poor has made more rapid advances within the last 20 years in this country than in the whole former period since the invention of printing.

During the eighteenth century attitudes towards educating the poor began to change. Charity schools supported by rich benefactors appeared around the country, although there was still a strong belief that it was dangerous to educate the masses. Therefore the emphasis in these schools was on obedience, respect for your superiors and a knowledge of the scriptures, with some practical skills suitable for work befitting your station in life.

For most of the century, Windsor had just one charity school for poor children, the Royal Free School founded in 1705 for 40 boys and 30 girls. The newspaper referred to it as the 'Charity School' or the 'Free School'. In 1813 it taught 90 boys and 20 girls in a schoolhouse in Church Street (now the Masonic Hall). 'Charity children' were carefully chosen by the trustees from respectable working class families, or the 'deserving' poor; in August 1813 they selected four boys and four girls from 34 applicants. The school was not entirely free, for children had to bring one penny a week for the 'Penny Club'. The curriculum was basic: when in June 1815 Sarah Muffett, mistress of the Windsor Charity School died at 77 after 30 years service the request for a new teacher read: 'Wanted, Mistress for the Charity School in Windsor to teach 20 girls reading, knitting and plain needlework'. The boys were taught reading, writing and reckoning, with some practical instruction in woodwork or similar crafts.

WANTED,

A MISTRESS, for the CHARITY SCHOOL of NEW WINDSOR, to teach Twenty Girls Reading, Knitting, and plain Needle-work. There are good Apartments for the Mistress to reside in, an Allowance of Coals, and a Salary of Twenty-Five Pounds a Year.

Any Person properly qualified may apply to Mr. EGELSTONE, of Windsor, Treasurer to the Charity, before the 4th of July next, on which Day a Meeting will be held for the Election, at Eleven o'Clock.

A middle aged Person, of the Established Church, without Incumbrance, will be preferred.

Satisfactory Reference, as to Character and Abilities, will be required.

The building of the Royal Free School,
founded in 1705,
is a Masonic Lodge in 2012

The school was supported by frequent gifts and money left in wills. Dr James Mingay left £800 to the Charity School in February 1813. In addition sermons were preached in the Parish Church for the benefit of the school. An 'impressive sermon' by the Rev. Philip Jennings in August 1813 raised £45, and £47 5s 6d was collected at the door after a sermon attended by Princess Augusta in October 1825.

'Charity children' benefitted from regular treats. The three-day perambulation of the Windsor boundary in May 1814 included the boys from the Charity School. There was wine and food provided each day en-route. They also took part in the parade celebrating peace in July 1814. In July 1816, the Queen gave children of the Charity and Sunday Schools plum cake and a glass of ale when the Princess Mary married the Duke of Gloucester.

By 1812, the Royal Free School was no longer the only charity school in the Windsor area. In 1785 the Ladies School had been founded in Peascod Street. One mention in the newspaper in November 1820 stated that 'the children belonging to the Ladies School in Peascod Street had a dinner of beef and plum-pudding, in honour of the Birthday of its most gracious Patroness her Royal Highness the Princess Augusta'. The school merged with the National School that same year.

Lady Harcourt's school In Clewer Green was endowed in 1806. Mary Countess Harcourt bequeathed £500 to the school in Hatch Lane, which catered for 80 boys and 70 girls. In Eton Mark Anthony Porny left a bequest for a 'permanent foundation' for the Charity and Sunday school established in 1790. Mr Tebbot completed the building for £1,723. There was also a small Catholic school, opened in 1828 in the Chapel in Hermitage Lane, although not mentioned in the newspaper. These all are still thriving schools, but are now free primary state schools.

There was a school in Old Windsor, set up in 1809 by Princess Elizabeth. On 15 August 1812 forty 'charity children' of Her Majesty's school dined in tents in Frogmore and in October Queen Charlotte and her daughters Elizabeth and Mary inspected their 'Female School of Industry' in Old Windsor.

Another school not reported in the newspaper until 1845 was a ragged school founded by a chimney sweep in George Street some time during the 1820s. It was the only school that would educate, feed and clothe the dirty and shoeless ragamuffins of Windsor, which no other schools accepted. It would become a very important charity in Windsor with its own schoolhouse in Oxford Road, until compulsory education was introduced in 1871.

Sunday Schools

Sunday schools were also well established in Windsor by 1812. Charity schools in Windsor were under the auspices of the established church, and would only take pupils belonging to the Church of England; the Sunday schools were a vital aspect of the dissenting churches and the only way poor children whose parents did not belong to the established church could gain access to education. However, Windsor and Clewer parish churches soon set up Sunday schools which were principally aimed at the poorer children in the town and children who worked all week. There was no need for a schoolhouse, as children were taught in the churches. In January 1813 the *Express* reported that the committee of the Sunday School of Windsor held their first AGM. Two hundred children had been clothed and educated from the Penny Club of the children and the 'subscriptions of the benevolent'. But they also benefitted from sermons in the Parish Church; £61 13s was collected at the door in August 1815.

National School

But there were still many children in Windsor without access to education in 1812. When it was announced during a sermon at the Parish Church in October 1818, that a National School was to be built 'for the advantage of the large population of this town', Charles Knight father and son were among the first to contribute. The National School Society had been founded in 1811 to promote the teaching of the poor in accordance with the Church of England. It was the first attempt to bring education to the masses and to standardise teaching, with regular inspections.

The school started immediately with 185 children from Windsor, 58 from Clewer and 55 from other areas. The boys were taught in auction rooms and the girls in a Sunday-school room in Peascod Street while a schoolhouse was built to accommodate 200 boys and 200 girls. Land was secured in 'Maids' Acre' at the bottom of Peascod Street, (now St Leonard's Road) and the foundation stone was laid on 20 October 1819 by Major General Sir Herbert Taylor and Mr Edward Hawke Locker.

Like the Free School, the National School received donations from well-wishers, and money was collected at the church door after special sermons. The AGM in January 1821 held at the Town-Hall was the first to be reported in the paper. It stated that £1,190 had been raised for the school building, and £384 3s 9½d were received in donations and subscriptions.

The school thrived; at the AGM in January 1823 it was noted that there were 309 children on the books, in 1824 there were 405, 100 more than in 1820. The annual salary of the master and mistress was £120.

The Rev. G Champagne set up an endowment for the school, a 'most praiseworthy and judicious benevolence'. After the annual examinations in March 1825, 'fourteen boys and girls most distinguished for their knowledge of the Scriptures' received seven shillings and a 'Champagne Bible' during a ceremony attended by dignitaries, parents, governors and children.

The National School children were also given treats. In November 1823, 400 children sat down for a meal 'in honour of the King taking up residence in the Castle' and the new Mayor Robert Tebbot 'regaled the girls of the National School with buns and ale' in Bachelors' Acre in October 1828.

The National School merged with the Royal Free School in 1859 when they moved to the Bachelors' Acre site.

Private education

There were a number of private fee-paying schools in Windsor; and after the French wars, new schools seemed to appear with frequent regularity. Anyone could set up a school without questions asked or inspections made. Miss Smith announced a new boarding and day school for young ladies in Park Street (March 1813), and Miss Sharman proposed to open a day school for young ladies at her father's house in Castle Street in January 1815.

A school for children from four to eight, at six pence per week, was started by A Davis at 3 Church Street in April 1817. Eight establishments announced the new terms of their schools in the newspaper in January 1819. Of these, Miss Sharman gave her charges to be £31 10s per annum for board with English, Fancy Work, &c, and 'each lady to bring a silver spoon and six towels'.

Mrs Penn's establishment, Windsor Park House at Datchet, offered board and education including 'washing, English, French, music, writing, arithmetic and geography with the globe', also 'warm and cold shower bath for the use of the young ladies if required', all for 33 guineas per annum. Grove House school in St Leonard's Road was first mentioned in March 1824: 'The young gentlemen at Grove House School are instructed in gymnastics, we have no doubt the system will be eagerly adopted in the neighbourhood'. In January 1825 a new day school for young gentlemen was opened by Mr J L Binfield at 13 Church Street.

Some schools expanded; in January 1819 Mr Phillips moved his school from High Street to St Albans Street, 'which has an extensive playground', and the Misses Englefield moved their school from Park Street to a larger house in High Street in January 1829.

Some schools did not last very long; in December 1824 Mr Gresley's boarding school at Datchet Common sold 25 bedsteads and feather beds, furniture, plate, linen etc and 'a cow in calf, a sow and three piglets'. The house was for 'lease or let'. A school in Peascod Street opposite the Crown Inn sold all of its effects, including brewing utensils, when it closed in March 1818.

But there were schools around the country that seemed to come straight out of a Dickens' novel. In January 1824 the newspaper reported in a long and detailed editorial from the Court of the King's Bench on a law-suit, brought against Mr Scarlett, master of a Yorkshire school by a London builder who had sent his sons there. He maintained 'that the boys 'slept in a cock-loft, that they slept eight in a bed, exposed to the weather; that their food was unwholesome; that they were devoured by vermin and the itch'. Another witness claimed 'the boys were treated more like pigs than Christians'. Mr Scarlett was fined £150. Dotheboys Hall in *Nicholas Nickleby* was much like this school.

Few of these private schools have survived in the Windsor area, with one notable exception:

Eton College

Eton College, established in 1440 by Henry VI for 70 poor scholars, enjoyed some notoriety during this period. Dr Keate, headmaster 1809-1834, was renowned for trying to establish discipline and was not averse to using the cane. In October 1815 the *Express* reported:

> On Monday, five young gentlemen of Eton School, in a frolicsome mood, performed the ceremony which they call making a 'boy free of the school', by tying him to the posts of a bed and gagging his mouth in such a manner, as almost to occasion strangulation.

All five refused to 'submit to be flogged' and were ordered to quit the school, 'on pains of being disgraced by a public expulsion'. A more serious disturbance occurred in November 1818 after which seven scholars were expelled, and two left privately. The newspaper did not give details or names but only reported:

...a serious interruption of the usual good order that distinguishes the first public school of the country...many of the scholars of Eton College have united to resist the discipline of the institution and to assail the proper objects of their reverence and esteem with wilful dis respect.

Every year on 4 June the College celebrated the birthday of George III, their most revered patron, with a regatta. In 1817 they celebrated the King's 79th birthday with the 'usual aquatic procession to Surly Hall', followed by a meal and fireworks in the evening. The tradition was carried on after the death of the King, and today takes place on the Wednesday before the first weekend in June. In 1828 the *Express* reported that the gentlemen of Eton held their annual regatta in commemoration of the late King's birthday on June 4, and 'the procession was accompanied by the band of the 2nd Life Guards'; the band of the Grenadier Guards was moored below the bridge 'and produced a beautiful effect', but it brought them unfortunately into the line of fire and smoke from the fireworks. 'It was evident, however that they knew how to stand fire for they continued to play with the greatest nonchalance and good humour'.

Eton Montem

The Montem, another Eton tradition, but long since discontinued, was held three times a year. The boys processed in fancy costume 'ad montem' (to the mount), a small hill in Slough. It was another celebration relished by George III, and George IV carried on the tradition his father enjoyed. In May 1826 the newspaper reported that:

Eton Montem was celebrated with great splendour. The bands of the 1st Life Guards and 63rd Regiment played. The King was absent, but sent 100 guineas. The Persian and Spanish costumes of the young gentlemen were especially commended. A ball in the evening at the Town Hall was well attended.

George IV tried to ingratiate himself with Eton; he presented a set of classical authors for the use of the scholars, each elegantly bound and with his crest, and asked for an annual holiday to be given to them in commemoration of the gift.

Eton College was not unaware of the poverty in the neighbourhood. In December 1813 coal and potatoes were procured by the College to be sold to the poor at reduced prices; in 1823 the college supplied coal, soup, bread and Christmas dinner to the inhabitants of Eton. Both masters and boys regularly contributed to appeals and were generous in their charitable giving. The Provost and Fellows of Eton College funded a new chapel for the people of Eton, completed in 1820.

A number of Eton College tragedies were reported in the newspaper. In July 1815 Benjamin Treby Hayes drowned in the Thames swimming too close to the weir. Another Eton boy was floating paper boats down a swollen brook in December 1822. He slipped and was carried away; this was a double tragedy, as his elder brother had been killed by gunpowder at the school on 5 November some twelve years earlier. In March 1821 William Wright, aged nine, died when his nightshirt caught fire as he stood in front of the hearth reading his mother's letter. Just as tragic was the case of F A Cooper who was killed in a fight with two other Eton boys. He was buried in the Chapel at Eton College; Dr Keate read the service. The boys responsible for the tragedy, Wood and Leith, were accused of manslaughter and tried at the assizes. They were acquitted as all three witnesses failed to appear.

Eton scholars were not always very prompt in settling their bills. The following notice appeared on the front page of the *Express* in July 1829:

Eton College

The Noblemen and Gentlemen, late Students of the above royal Establishment, are earnestly solicited by N C Tomkins, to settle their long standing money accounts, and for want of their addresses is obliged to communicate through the public press and shall be very sorry to be under the necessity of proceeding any further in a public manner by an unpleasant exposure.

Surely just an oversight!

The Rebuilding of Windsor Parish Church

Windsor Parish Church as it was in 1812
The Bodleian Libraries, The University of Oxford Shelfmark: MS. Top,c.51,fol.194

Windsor's original medieval parish church was erected around 1130 and stood on the site of the present-day church. The medieval church had several side chapels and a low central tower (which by 1479 had a clock). In the sixteenth century a wooden structure was added to the tower, which contained bells and had a spire.

The last major piece of work to be carried out in the old building was the construction of the North Gallery. A notice in the *Windsor Express* in 1812 reported that the gallery was 'now completely finished; many persons had already taken their allotted seats there' and that the 'excellence of the workmanship does great credit to Messrs Trigg & Son of Eton, builders'.

Over the centuries it was frequently being patched up. In June 1815 there was a Vestry Meeting to discuss plans to raise funds for 'putting the church into substantial repair' as parts of the building, the tower and the belfry, in particular, were in a very dilapidated state. It was resolved to meet the costs of repair by voluntary subscription. Even before the money had been raised the tower and belfry were too far-gone to warrant repair. In August 1815, the tower was dismantled and taken down. The materials were sold by auction on 9 September 1815 by Mr Fennell who had offices in Windsor High Street. An advertisement in the *Express* states that

119

> The remains of the Tower of the Parish Church... lately taken down and now lying part in the churchyard and part in the stable-yard belonging to the Castle Inn consisted of a large quantity of oak timber...7,000 building bricks, 40 loads of flints; 50 loads of large chalk and 96 loads of mortar and chalk rubbish.

In October 1818, a survey of the fabric was conducted by the architect Lewis Wyatt, who concluded in his report, that 'the very dilapidated state' of the church 'would render any further repair inefficient'. At the next Vestry meeting the Parishioners of Windsor unanimously voted that steps should be taken to 'to provide for the erection of a New Church'. A committee was established to start the process of finding funding for the new building.

The *Windsor Express* of 27 December 1818 published a list of some 87 names of the great and good of the Windsor community. At the top of the list Windsor MP John Ramsbottom had contributed the very generous sum of £500. Other early contributors included Charles Knight who had given £30, James Bedborough £20 and John Caley £10. Subscriptions continued to be collected right up to the completion in the church. In early 1820 money was received from the Royal family which included £500 from George III shortly before his death, the Prince Regent £200 and £100 each from the Duke of Cambridge and the Princesses Augusta and Sophia. By April 1820 £5299 had been collected. It was later resolved that a further £4000 in parish rates would go to the fund.

In May of 1819 there were rumours floating around the town that the new building was to be on Bachelors' Acre. This rumour was quashed by the editors of the paper who explained that 'no idea of placing the new church in the Bachelors' Acre had ever been contemplated by the committee' and that 'the building will be erected as near as possible on the site of the present church'.

The Committee for the Rebuilding of the Parish Church announced in the *Windsor Express* in February 1820 that they were 'intending to proceed with all possible dispatch towards forwarding the rebuilding of the Parish Church'. The committee also requested that people who wanted to have monuments and memorials transferred to the new church should give notice to the Vicar and Churchwardens, together with the stone mason they wanted to employ to take them down. They were removed in July 1820 prior to the demolition of the church.

The architect chosen was Charles Hollis who used the newly discovered process of cast iron in the construction. Between May and July 1820 advertisements were run in the *Express* by Hollis requesting builders to present tenders. The lowest tender of £9390 was accepted for the work and the contract went to local builders James Bedborough and Robert Tebbott who had their yard in Sheet Street.

Once the contract had been signed the church was demolished and materials were sold by Mr Tebbott in St Alban's Street adjacent to the churchyard. The sale took place on Wednesday 30 August and consisted of rubble, beams and rafters, 1000 roofing tiles and wrought iron.

In September 1820 the cornerstone of the new church was to be laid by the Duke of York as part of a Masonic ceremony. At the last minute the Duke was unable to attend, so MP John Ramsbottom deputised for him. Ramsbottom was also a very senior freemason. A report in the *Express* dated 17 September 1820 describes the Masonic procession from the Guildhall to the site which was led by Clergy from both St George's Chapel and the Parish Church. They were followed by visiting Freemasons and members of the Rebuilding Committee. Next in the procession was the foundation stone itself accompanied by the architect Charles Hollis and builders James Bedborough and Robert Tebbott, followed by the Mace Bearer and the Mayor, George Davis, and members of the Corporation of New Windsor. At the rear of the procession was John Ramsbottom and other Grand Officers of the United Grand Lodge of England. The ceremony was carried out with full Masonic pomp and circumstance: the newspaper reports that 'over one hundred Freemasons were present at the ceremony'.

By August 1821 the church had been roofed and was nearing completion. The contractors were paid their second instalment of money. The *Express* said that 'The external appearance of the building is particularly neat, and the execution reflects the highest credit on all concerned in the work'. In October the last stone pinnacles were added to the tower, watched by those Windsorians who dared to venture up to the top of the tower. To enable the plaster of the walls to dry out completely the walls were not painted until May 1824

On Tuesday 18 June 1822 at 11am the church was consecrated by the Bishop of Salisbury. There was a procession from the Town Hall to the Parish Church led by the boys and girls of the Free School and the girls of the Queen's School. Next in line was the Corporation of New Windsor, the clergy, and inhabitants. The consecration was followed by the service of holy communion led by the Bishop. In September that year the Parish Church received the Royal gift of two high oak chairs from Princess Augusta. They had originally been commissioned by Queen Charlotte for her chapel at Kew.

In January 1823 the sound of the church bells was heard for the first time since the demolition of the tower in 1815. The same bells ring out from the Parish Church to this day.

In May 1824 the church was closed whilst painting took place and did not open until August that year. The *Express* of 7 August 1824 describes the newly painted church:

> The pews and galleries are painted of a brilliant light wainscot,
> and the walls of a neat stone colour. A tasteful Gothic embellishment of
> plaster has been placed over the painting at the altar. (EK)

Other Churches in Windsor

Beside the parish church of St John the Baptist, there was the parish church of St Andrew in Clewer. These two Anglican churches did not have the capacity to hold all parishioners of Windsor and Clewer at their services on Sunday, furthermore, the pew charges excluded all but the wealthy. The need for new churches was expressed in an official document printed in the *Express* in March 1818. It stated that in parishes in England 'containing a Population above 2,000... the excess of population above the capacity of churches and chapels is 3,710,564'. There was an appeal for a new church for Clewer in July 1818 as 'parishioners living in the Goswell area can not get to church during much of the year because of flooding'. Even the re-building of the Windsor Parish church did not supply enough pews: it had a capacity of 1,654, with only 308 free seats. Clewer Church had seating for 500.

It was partly the lack of pews, partly the persuasive preaching of dissenting ministers and partly the attitude of the Church of England towards the poor that drove many towards the dissenting churches. A Congregational church was known to have existed in Windsor in 1777, started by a soldier who preached sermons in a cottage in Sun Passage, but there was no permanent building till 1832. Methodist worship goes back to 1756 in Windsor when John Wesley preached here, but in 1800 another soldier called John Ould started regular Methodist meetings in Windsor, and a Methodist church had been established in Bier Lane before 1812.

In May 1814 William Ratcliff, drummer of the West Kent Militia preached a sermon at the Methodist meeting in Windsor from John iii, 14,15. 'The unassuming deportment, pleasing address, eloquent and appropriate stile of this young man drew the marked attention of a numerous and very respectable audience'.

A Dissenter's meeting-house was mentioned in the paper in January 1813. In 1814 the former Windsor theatre in High Street became a chapel for the Independent Church, established in 1805. In September 1814, two sermons were preached on the day of opening. The following year the first anniversary was celebrated with two services, the 'congregation was numerous and respectable' and £44 7s was collected. The church had raised £600 in Windsor and £500 from the neighbourhood, to turn the theatre into a chapel. This was a statement of a flourishing and successful community, and yet none of the children of dissenters had access to Church of England schools.

Another place of worship in Windsor was a small Catholic Chapel in Hermitage Lane, but it is not mentioned in the newspaper during this period, there was still too much anti-Catholic feeling. The chapel was built by Felix Riley, according to the wishes of his father John, and registered at the Newbury Quarter Session in April 1826. John Riley was a prominent and respected citizen, who had a private chapel in his house in Peascod Street. There was an obituary to him in the newspaper when he died aged 78:

> ...by the poor his loss will be severely felt, his charities being most extensively dispensed; humanity and liberality of sentiment were the leading features of his character, and his benevolence and bountiful hand was at all times open to every call of distress both public and private'. (May 1817)

Prior to the chapel in Hermitage Lane, a room in the Hope Inn in Frogmore had been used to celebrate the Catholic mass by Abbé Noel Duclos of Evreux, a French émigré who taught at Eton College. He died in Eton in 1831 at the age of 81 and is buried in the churchyard there.

By the mid-nineteenth century there were four Anglican churches, five Dissenting churches and one Catholic Church in Windsor and Clewer, but average attendance according to the Ecclesiastical Census of 1851 was just 55.6% of the population.

Catholic Emancipation

One of the burning political issues of the early nineteenth century was the question of Catholic emancipation. Although draconian legislation of the seventeenth century had been eased and Roman Catholics could now worship as they wished, anti-Catholic laws and prejudice remained. If you were a Catholic you were a second-class citizen, unable to take high public office, such as in the judiciary, or to be a Member of Parliament. This was especially resented in Ireland where the majority of the population was Catholic.

The argument for reform gained fresh momentum after the Union with Ireland in 1801. William Pitt, the Prime Minister then, had promised relief for the Catholic population in return for their agreement to Ireland joining the pre-existing union of England, Wales and Scotland. His inability to keep that promise in the teeth of implacable opposition from George III (who claimed that Catholic emancipation was contrary to his Coronation oath) led to renewed Catholic protests in England and further unrest in Ireland.

The early editions of the *Windsor Express* contained accounts of the various petitions for and against Catholic emancipation, which were debated with considerable passion in both the Commons and the Lords.

The Tory government in power in 1812 when the paper was launched was divided on the issue. Most of the Lords, led by the Lord Chancellor, Eldon, were opposed to Emancipation; in the Commons Robert Peel, Chief Secretary for Ireland, was opposed, though George Canning was in favour. A Relief Bill, introduced in 1813, which would have enabled Roman Catholics to sit in either House of Parliament after swearing an oath, was defeated by four votes, the proceedings in Parliament duly reported in the May editions of the paper. There was equal coverage of the Roman Catholic Relief Bill of 1821. This Bill, which would have afforded provision to the Roman Catholic clergy, was passed by the Commons but rejected by the Lords owing to Eldon's opposition, and the intransigent stand taken by the Duke of York, whose speech against allowing Roman Catholics to participate in politics was reported (22 April):

> HRH the Duke of York declared that he rose to address their Lordships, not without the greatest reluctance and with considerable pain. He felt it an imperative duty to *Express* what he thought, when their Lordships were called upon to sanction a measure that might produce an entire change in those great principles which marked the Revolution of 1688

that he trusted he was no enemy to toleration in its proper sense; but there was certainly a wide difference between extending to Roman Catholics the liberty of conscience in the performance of sacred rites and allowing them to partake in political sway.

Henceforth, the opponents of emancipation relied on the Crown and Lords to check the movement. In 1822 and 1823, the Lords again threw out partial Relief Bills which had been passed by the Commons. The 1822 Bill to allow Roman Catholic Peers to sit in the House, passed by the Commons, was defeated by a majority of 42 (29 June 1822). This was followed by petitions against any further concessions to Roman Catholics (19 April 1823). A further Bill, to render the English Roman Catholics eligible to certain offices and restore the elective franchise to Roman Catholics, was opposed by the Bishops and thrown out by the Lords (29 May 1824).

On Saturday 25 April (reported in the *Express* for 30 April 1825), the Duke of York again addressed the House of Lords:

> You place the Church of England in a situation in which no other church in the world is placed; the Roman Catholic will not allow the Church of England, or Parliament, to interfere with his church and yet he requires you to allow him to Interfere with your church and to legislate for it.

The Duke went on to say that he spoke as an individual:

> But consider, my Lords, the situation in which you place the sovereign. By the Coronation Oath, the sovereign is bound to maintain the church established in her doctrine, discipline and rites inviolate – and in every situation in which I may be placed, I will maintain them, so help me God.

It was disorder in Ireland that finally forced the issue. The Irish Catholics now had a new leader, Daniel O'Connell, who in 1823 formed the Catholic Association to coerce the British government. On 12 June 1828, the *Express* informed its readers that Mr O'Connell had been elected to represent Clare in Parliament with a majority of 1075 votes over his Protestant landowning opponent, Vesey Fitzgerald. As the law now stood he was ineligible to take his seat. A refusal to change the law would aggravate an already serious situation. The *Express*'s account (1 November 1828) of a run on the Wexford Branch of the Bank of Ireland 'because the manager is a "Brunswicker" and anti Catholic', demonstrated that the issue of Catholic emancipation was not only embittering social relations; it was also hampering commerce. On 10 May the paper had carried a claim that the Catholic Bill could never succeed because 'The King' (George IV) 'would rather lay his head upon the scaffold than violate his sworn duty to his people', but staunch opponents like Robert Peel and the Duke of Wellington (now Prime Minister) were pragmatists; they recognised that on the issue of Catholic emancipation principle would have to serve the interests of political stability and social cohesion.

Early the following year, the *Express* printed Wellington's answer to a letter from Dr Curtis, Catholic Primate of Ireland, in support of settlement of the Roman Catholic question. Throughout January and February 1829 readers were kept abreast of the arguments for and against emancipation being debated in Parliament, enlivened by a little local flavour. The edition for 21 February told of a stir caused by a rumour that Daniel O'Connell was lodging at the White Hart – but it was only his brother John! On 7 March the paper presented an article on the absurdity of the vulgar prejudices against the Catholics. On 11 April it was able to announce that 'The Catholic Relief Bill was carried last night by a majority of 140 votes and will receive the Royal Assent' (Wellington had threatened to resign if the King withheld his consent). It was not a good week for the Duke who was attacked in St James's Park by John Appleyard who claimed to be the real descendant of Henry VIII, or for Robert Peel. Both men had put pragmatism before principle. Wellington assuaged his remorse by fighting a duel with Lord Winchilsea [see article on *Duels*]; Peel resigned. 'Few politicians', thundered the *Express*,' have been so intensely hated as Mr Peel, a consequence of his dithering and his inability to make clear choices' (11 July 1829).

The Roman Catholic Emancipation Act of April 1829, provided that Roman Catholics should be eligible for all public offices, except those of Regent, Lord Chancellor of England and Ireland, Lord Lieutenant of Ireland and judicial appointments in ecclesiastical courts. Members of Parliament were no longer required to abjure Roman Catholic doctrines. They were to deny on oath the legality of papal jurisdiction in the British Isles, to deny that papal jurisdiction justified the deposition or murder of a sovereign. Jesuits and monks were not to enter the country without licence. At the same time an Act was passed raising the qualification for the franchise in Ireland from 40s to £10 in the hope that the dangerous power of the peasantry would be weakened. But opposition was not stifled: the extreme Tories, especially Eldon, declared that the Government had 'run away from its principles like a pack of cowards'. (SM)

War and Peace

The Garrison

The newspaper was much preoccupied with the soldiers stationed in the Windsor Garrison and gives regular updates of regiments moving in and out of the town. Windsor's relationship with its soldiers was not always harmonious, but both good and negative stories were reported in the press.

Two large barracks had been built in the town during the wars with France, turning Windsor into a major garrison town. Previously soldiers had been quartered in public houses or in the Castle, especially if they came as the escort of the sovereign.

The Cavalry Barracks, often referred to as Horse Barracks or Spital Barracks, were occupied by the Royal Horse Guards, The Blues, George III's favourite regiment. They left Windsor in June 1821. The newspaper wrote:

> ... the occasion of the Royal Regiment of Horse Guards, Blue, quitting Windsor, after having been stationed in this Town, with few intervals, for 17 years, demands a public testimony of the Inhabitants of the Borough, to the uniform liberality and kindness of the Officers, and the marked integrity and good order of the Men, of that distinguished Regiment.

This was followed by the public address made by the Mayor John Banister, in which he stressed that the regiment contributed to the welfare and amusement of the town. Probably most welcomed by the men were three barrels of excellent ale, presented by Windsor brewer Messrs Jennings. Thereafter the two regiments of Life Guards and the Royal Horse Guards did a one-year tour of duty in Windsor and two in London. Occasionally the Dragoons were stationed there briefly.

The Infantry Barracks, also called Foot Barracks or Sheet Street Barracks were built on one acre of land between Sheet Street and Barrack Lane, formerly an orchard belonging to Mr E Pinnock. It was flanked to the north by an alms-house and to the south by the Windsor Poor House, which had been built as a Pest House in 1769. During the first half of the nineteenth century the Infantry Barracks were occupied not only by the Foot Guards, but by a whole range of Infantry Regiments. For 13 years of the war the barracks were occupied by the Staffordshire Militia, while the regular army was fighting abroad.

The Staffordshire Militia 1804

Courtesy of the National Army Museum

In December 1813 it was reported that 300 men from the Staffordshire Militia stationed in Windsor joined the Foot Guards and the 4th Regiment.

In October 1814, just before the Staffordshires left Windsor, Mrs Gor-Langton, wife of the Colonel of the Oxfordshire Militia gave a dinner at the Town Hall for 150 wives and children of soldiers.

In November 1812 the 29th Regiment had come to Windsor from Portugal a 'skeleton of a regiment'. Many men from the Militia were eager to enrol 'in this band of heroes'. In December the *Windsor and Eton Express* published the history of two cavalry horses belonging to Colonel Way of the 29th Regiment, one called *Suwarrow,* which once belonged to the Grand Vizier of Turkey, and the other *Black Jack* who had briefly been captured by the French; after it was rescued, it carried the colonel in several battles against the French.

The regiment endeared itself to the people of Windsor when they read that every officer and soldier had given a day's pay for their brother soldiers who were prisoners of war in France. When the 29th left for Spain in February 1813 a grand ball was given at the Town Hall for the officers; and the ladies and gentlemen of the town made a collection of £45 19s to help the poor women and children who could not accompany their husbands.

The regular army returned to Windsor after the Battle of Waterloo. Windsorians turned out in great numbers to greet and cheer the soldiers as they marched into town. The first to return in January 1816 were the Grenadier Guards. As they marched into Windsor headed by the Duke of York, they were cheered by the populace and decorated with laurels. In February the Royal Horse Guards were greeted by Sir Robert Hill on entering Park Street. In April soldiers of both the Grenadier Guards and Horse Guards received their Waterloo medals in Windsor. The same issue reported that 200 soldiers of the Coldstream Guards stationed in France, were severely afflicted with ophthalmia (Conjunctivitis).

Windsorians enjoyed the pomp and ceremony of their regiments. There were frequent military parades and reviews in the Great Park and regimental bands played regularly in the Long Walk, and on the terrace of Windsor Castle.

Officers were often wined and dined by local people. In July 1814 Mrs Buckner gave a party at Clewer Villa to the gentry and officers of both regiments stationed in Windsor, while the band of the 5th Regiment played. There were also many public dinners for officers and the men, especially on the anniversary of Waterloo in June. On the first anniversary 600 soldiers were regaled with roast beef, mutton and veal, ham and meat pies, wine and ale in the Long Walk, while the officers dined with the Duke of York; in the evening there was a ball in the Town Hall.

But the regiments knew how to return the compliment. In June 1817 the Royal family and members of the nobility attended a ball at the riding school in the Cavalry Barracks. The supper was served by Mr Layton, and Mr Tebbot provided the decorations (both were at some time Mayors of Windsor). The bands of the Royal Horse Guards and the Grenadier Guards played.

The people of Windsor were also grateful for the help given by soldiers. In August 1822 soldiers from the 7th Regiment were praised for helping to pump water from the river to lay secure foundations for the last pier of the new bridge. Between 40 and 60 soldiers worked four hourly shifts to work four chain pumps.

Fires

Soldiers also helped to put out fires. Each barracks had its own fire engine. 'Six fine engines attended at a fire' in April 1818 at Mr Jacobs' silversmith in Thames Street, but the efforts of the Royal Horse Guards and Grenadier Guards to contain the fire were particularly mentioned. At the same time it was stated that a regular fire-service was needed in Windsor.

In April 1822 a fire, which started in Charles Knight's stables in Sheet Street, soon spread to adjoining tenements occupied by 72 persons. Soldiers from the nearby barracks were first on the scene and managed to save three of the eight tenements and Mr Knight's stable and coach house. But 16 families were made homeless. Charles Knight immediately started a subscription list for the destitute families, which raised over £270 in two weeks. Mr Knight thanked Colonel De Burgh and the officers and men of the regiments on duty in Windsor 'for the very great exertion with which they attempted to check the progress of the flames'.

In May 1823 a fire started at the premises of a stationer in Castle Street only 30 feet from the Castle wall and next to the premises recently vacated by Mr Caley. It destroyed five houses. The flames were only stopped by Mr O'Riley's brick built dwelling. Again the soldiers were praised for their bravery in putting out the fire, and the need was expressed again for a body of firemen. The turncock for Windsor's only fire engine in Church Street, lived in Eton.

But things did not always go smoothly. In May 1819, five privates of the 3rd Regiment were charged with stealing from a house while putting out a fire. The following week it was reported that one of them was charged with stealing a pocket handkerchief, while the other four had been released.

FIRE IN CASTLE-STREET.

PRESENT SUBSCRIPTIONS.

	£	s.	d.
H.R.H. The Princess Augusta	5	5	0
The Mayor and Corporation	5	5	0
The Dean and Canons	10	10	0
The Phoenix Fire-Office	10	10	0
Norwich Union Fire Office, per Mr. Barton, Eton	5	5	0
Sun Fire Office, per W.Voules, Esq.	10	10	0
County Fire Office, per Mr. D. Smith	5	5	0
Royal Exchange Fire Office, per W. Long, Esq.	5	0	0
Hope Fire Office	5	0	0

	£	s.	d.		£	s.	d.
J. Ramsbottom, Esq. M. P.	5	5	0	Mr. Millns	1	0	0
Edw. Disbrowe, Esq. M. P.	5	5	0	Mr. B. Brown	1	0	0
John Chapman, Esq.	2	0	0	Mr. Alder	1	0	0
Charles Hayes, Esq.	5	5	0	Sharman and Son	2	0	0
Mr. Jenner	1	0	0	Mr. Berridge	1	0	0
Mr. C. Snowden	1	0	0	J. Egelstone, Esq.	1	0	0
J. O'Reilly, Esq.	2	0	0	Knight and Son	1	0	0
Mr. Wright	1	0	0	Knight and Dredge	1	0	0
Mr. John Clode	1	0	0	Mr.Jones,Grove-house	1	0	0
Mr. W. Clode	1	0	0	Mr. C. Layton, jun.	1	0	0
Mr. D. Smith	1	0	0	Mr. F. W. Davis	1	0	0
Mr. Goertz	?	0	0	Inmates at Messrs. Sharman and Son's	0	12	6
Mr. John Brown	1	0	0	Major Sturges	1	0	0
Mr. Cooper, High-st.	1	0	0	Mr. Tebbott	1	0	0
Mr. J. Clode, Church-street	1	0	0	Mrs. C. Buckeridge	1	0	0
Mr. Thos. Jennings	2	0	0	Mr. Barton, Eton	0	10	0
Mr. Church	2	0	0	Wm. Legh, Esq.	2	0	0
John Secker, Esq.	2	0	0	Miss Cooper, Cloisters	1	0	0
Mr. R. Clode	1	0	0	Mr.J. Barton, High-st.	0	5	0
Mr. T. Adams, Peas-cod-street	1	0	0	Mr. Ray	1	0	0
Mr.Caley, High-st.	1	0	0	Mrs. Dawson,Cloisters	1	0	0
Mrs. Kennicott	1	1	0	Mr.E.Bovingdon, jun.	1	0	0
Miss Jeffreys	1	1	0	Mr. Edward Smith	1	0	0
Mrs. Kennedy	0	10	0	Mrs. Hallam	1	0	0
Miss C. Cooper, High-street	1	0	0	Miss Hallam	1	0	0
Mrs. Lockman	3	0	0	Mrs. Phillips and Son	1	0	0
Mr. Burtt, Peascod-street	1	0	0	Mr. Henry Griesbach	0	10	0
Messrs. Atkins and Son	1	0	0	Miss Blakeney	0	10	0
R. Battiscombe, Esq.	2	0	0	Rev. C. B. Sumner	1	1	0
Mr. Twinch, Church-lane	0	10	6	Rev. I. Gosset	3	0	0
Mr. Lovegrove	1	0	0	Mr. Agnew	1	0	0
Rev. Mr. Redford	1	0	0	Mrs. Margaret Hayes	1	1	0
Miss Roberts, Sarum Tower	1	0	0	Mr. Webster, Castle	0	5	0
Miss Henley	1	1	0	Miss Cantrell	0	10	0
Mrs. M'Nab	1	0	0	Mr. Coombs	1	1	0
Mr. Ritchie	0	10	0	Mr. Hanson	1	0	0
Lieutenant Johnson	0	10	0	Colonel Kinsey	1	0	0
W. de St. Croix, Esq.	1	0	0	Mr. Cartwright	0	10	0
Mr. Portus, Castle	0	10	0	Mrs.Adkin,St.Alban's street	0	10	0
Mr. Banbridge	0	10	0	Mr.Hall,Datchet-lane	0	10	0
Mr. Teede	0	5	0	Mrs. Pine	1	0	0
Mr. Sanders	0	10	0	Miss Pine	1	0	0
General Spencer	1	0	0	Miss Pennington	0	10	0
Mr. Banister	1	0	0	Inmates at Mr. Caley's	0	18	0
Mr. Blunt	1	0	0	Mr. Cutt	1	0	0
Mr. Adams, Castle-st.	1	0	0	Misses Secker	1	0	0
Mr. T. Woolridge, Mr. Church's	0	10	6	Mrs. M'Bean	0	10	0
Mr. Hewitt, Peascod-street	1	0	0	Mr. Snowden, Castle-street	0	10	0
John Ramsbottom,Esq.	2	0	0	Mrs.Angelo, Eton College	1	0	0
Mr. Wells	0	10	6	Mr.Frowd	0	10	0
Mr. W. Wells	0	10	6	Mr. H. Frowd	0	10	0
The Hon. and Rev, William Long	2	0	0	Mr. H. Emlyn	1	0	0
Mr. Tarver	0	10	0	Mrs. Thomas	5	0	0
W. J. Voules, Esq.	1	1	0	Mr. Delamain	1	0	0
				W. and L. Mason	1	0	0
				William Long, Esq.	1	1	0
				Dr. Fergusson	1	1	0
				John Snowden, Esq.	1	0	0
				Mr. Perkins (Flemish Farm	1	0	0
				Mr. Perryman	1	0	0

WINDSOR AND ETON.

Brawls

There were frequent disagreements and brawls between the townspeople and soldiers or between the soldiers of the two regiments. The first one to be reported in the paper was an affray between a market gardener and three soldiers of the 39th Regiment, who had been stripping fruit from his garden in September 1812. During the confrontation one soldier was shot in the hand. The soldiers were handed over to the regiment where they were tried by military court-martial and flogged.

More serious were riots during the funeral of Queen Caroline in August 1821. Although this occurred in London the paper reported the incidents and the inquest the following week in full. Richard Honey was killed, shot by a soldier of the Life Guards during an affray near Cumberland Gate shortly after the funeral procession had passed. Witnesses tried unsuccessfully to identify the officer who fired the shots. At the inquest the action of the officer was justified thus: 'The rioters who threw stones at the soldiers were ill-looking ragamuffin rascals'.

Often brawls were between soldiers of the two regiments stationed in Windsor. In November 1827 a fight which started in the George IV public house, spilled out into the streets. Bayonets were drawn and an apprentice was wounded by a soldier of the 21st Regiment. What was it all about? A private of the 21st Regiment had insulted the wife of a corporal in the Life Guards. The following week the paper reported that two soldiers had been severely punished, and that bayonets will not be worn in future outside barracks.

Most brawls happened around public houses but it was not always the soldiers who were the aggressors. A 'disgraceful drunken brawl' between soldiers and civilians outside the White Hart left several soldiers badly hurt. Five civilians were arrested and the magistrate praised the soldiers for their conduct (16 August 1828).

Tension also flared when soldiers were billeted in the public houses of Windsor because the barracks were overcrowded. In July 1825 Trooper Richard Trees of the Life Guards was billeted at the Star and Garter. He assaulted Mr Dash, the landlord, with a poker. Trees had been told to leave the kitchen, which was not part of the quarters assigned to him.

Officers were not averse to a bit of unruly behaviour. The first issue of the newspaper reported on page 4 that an officer of the 23rd Light Dragoons rode his horse up 142 of the '100 steps' to the Cloisters. This was probably just a dare, but when Lt Blake of the 55th Regiment assaulted Captain Clune in the Streets of Windsor he faced a court martial and was dismissed.

Black soldiers

There were considerable numbers of black soldiers in British regiments during the early nineteenth century. Black slaves instantly gained their freedom by joining the British army. Many of these enlisted in the American colonies. The *Windsor Express* gives us some evidence of black soldiers in

Windsor, and shows that there was a degree of discrimination, which was not tolerated. In July 1814 Thomas Anslow was fined 5s and sentenced to 3 months imprisonment, and then find sureties for good behaviour, for assaulting Augustus Buchally, a black drummer in the 5th Regiment. Another black drummer, John Johnson of the Royal Horse Guards, only gained notoriety after he had died in the Windsor barracks and was buried in Clewer churchyard. Two resurrection men were caught trying to steal his body. William Hide and Thomas Smith had been seen in Windsor with a horse and cart acting suspiciously. They stayed at the Garter Inn on the night of the 20th January 1822 and went out at 11pm. The Clewer parish clerk, Edward Atkins, surprised the two men in the graveyard but they ran away. Atkins found the open grave and the body of Johnson nearby, wrapped in the coat of one of the men. Hide and Smith were convicted and sent to the House of Correction for three months.

Soldiers' wives

The British army was always followed by large numbers of camp-followers, mostly women and children who acted as washerwomen, cooks, sutlers and comforters. Only 6 out of 100 soldiers were allowed to bring their wives into barracks and take them abroad, even on campaign, but this was often ignored. In November 1818, when the rest of the army finally returned from France the newspaper reported: 'The English army is followed by an astonishing number of women and children. 1,409 women and 1,829 children have already embarked at Calais'.

During the early nineteenth century soldiers and their families made up between 25 and 30% of the population of Windsor. Many of these were women and children who followed the army 'off the strength', which means they were not accepted by the regiment. Often they were not married, or if married, without the consent of the Commanding Officer. The women had to fend for themselves, sleeping rough, begging or trying to claim poor relief, putting great stress on the resources of the town.

In April 1813 the newspaper reported the concern of Mr Eggleston, the Overseer of the Poor, about repaying the very heavy demands made on the rates by the wives and families of the Staffordshire Militia during their long stay in Windsor.

Some families had remained behind when the militia went home. The children of Mr Houlder, formerly of the Staffordshire Militia, had stolen 70 head of broccoli from a garden in Clewer in April 1818; the magistrate decided not to punish them as long as the family left the parish. This way they would not claim poor relief. Where were they to go? The idea was that they went to their parish of birth where they were entitled to relief, but they could claim travelling allowance on the way. In January 1815 two soldiers' wives were charged with defrauding the Overseer of the Poor at Staines by presenting false passes which would have entitled them to £3 allowance to help them get to their homes.

Occasionally the newspaper highlighted the plight of these women. In January 1813 it reported that 50 women of the 29th Regiment, whose men had left for Spain, had been left abandoned. Immediately the ladies and gentlemen of the town and the Castle made a collection of £45 19s to help the women to make their way back to Ireland. The ladies of the town also extended help to a drummer and his pregnant wife who were living in miserable conditions in Windsor, because they had married without permission (July 1829).

But when it came to an outbreak of a serious fever in the Infantry Barracks in 1826, the reporter was more concerned with the fact that the disease could spread into the town. In August 1826 the paper reported:

> We very much regret to state that a serious fever has during the last few weeks prevailed amongst the children belonging to the 63rd Regiment in the barracks at Windsor... considerable alarm has in consequence been felt by the inhabitants, that our own population, which is sufficiently crowded, may be thus exposed to a fearful contagion.

The 63rd Regiment had arrived in Windsor in May from Ireland with 796 rank and file, 263 women and 252 children, and crowded into the small Infantry Barracks designed for 750 men. By the time they left for service abroad in December 1826, 88 children had died, possibly from scarlet fever. The newspaper did not mention the children again until December 1826, when they copied a report from Portsmouth:

> The 63rd arrived at Portsmouth and immediately embarked on the 'Melville' which was towed out of harbour on Sunday. The poor soldiers' wives arrived in hundreds, having marched 26 miles a day in a deplorable condition; and the scene of distress at witnessing their husbands' departure was heartrending. Three children died from fatigue on the road on Saturday. The commissioner and Sir James Lyons have made the necessary arrangements to forward all the poor women and children to their homes.

From Salamanca to Waterloo

England had already been at war with France for nineteen years when Charles Knight established the *Windsor Express* in 1812. For the town's inhabitants the war had a particular immediacy. Windsor was the favoured home of the King and Royal Family, and therefore at the hub of society and political intelligence; it was also a garrison town. The paper regularly regaled its readers with news of troop movements within the town and hostilities abroad.

In 1812, the war was still dominated by Napoleon's successes, but all that was about to change. The British army had recently gained a foot-hold in Portugal in order to drive the French out of Spain. This Peninsular War was important because it weakened Napoleon's operations elsewhere and has been described as 'a veritable ulcer, the original source of all his misfortunes'. After the death of the Commander in Chief, Sir John Moore, at Corunna, Wellington, recalled from India, took his place and in 1812 was facing a large French army near Salamanca. For Napoleon, who had already embarked on the disastrous invasion of Russia, it was the beginning of the end; for Wellington, it was the start of a legend.

The second week of the paper's publication carried the news of Wellington's victory at Salamanca, but 'this agreeable news' had to wait for confirmation until the next week's edition, when 'the delay which has so agitated the public mind' was explained. 'The vessel which brought these glad tidings was obliged by adverse winds to put into Tenby, a port in South Wales' (a fitting reminder of how difficult it was to obtain accurate information in the days before modern communications). Comparing Wellington to a Marlborough, or a Nelson, and putting the battle on a par with Agincourt, the editor eulogised the victorious Commander: 'Wellington has added a name to the list of British worthies that will hang upon the lips of an admiring world when the bloated triumphs of a despotic conqueror receive their portion of merited shame'.

Meanwhile, Napoleon advanced on Moscow. A Russian defeat at Borodino, in which both sides lost 40,000 troops, proved a Pyrrhic victory for France. As the cruel Russian winter set in, the Russians retreated, burning their crops to deny sustenance to the enemy. In December 1812, the *Political Inquirer*, the column nearest to a modern editorial in the *Express,* assessed the consequences of the Russian debacle for the French:

On 22 June last, Bonaparte declared war against Moscow, but its inhabitants had fled, its stores were destroyed and its palaces and temples were in flames. The Destroyer was caught in his own toil. His resources were exhausted, famine and cold crept upon the exultation of his followers – then all the miseries of a hasty retreat through a dreary and desolated region.

The next edition reviewed the French army's return to Paris 'a herd of wretched wanderers ... Napoleon, a base dastardly fugitive. He deserted as he did in Egypt. He ran away, alone and in disguise'.

Throughout 1813, and into the following year, the *Express* chronicled the Allied advances. In the Peninsula, Wellington's victory at Vittoria cleared Central Spain of the French, whilst Lieutenant Graham's capture of San Sebastian by storm, facilitated the advance into France. Wellington again defeated the French at the Battle of the Pyrenees (July 1813), and pursued the retreating enemy over the border and onto French territory. British successes at Vivelle (November 1813) Nive (December 1813) and Orthez (February 1814), completed the campaign. Elsewhere in Europe, Napoleon, his prestige impaired by the Russian campaign and Wellington's successes, had been defeated at the Battle of Leipzig. On 31 March 1814, the Allies entered Paris. Napoleon abdicated and was sent to the Island of Elba, while the victorious powers met at the Congress of Vienna to establish the future structure of Europe.

In Windsor, the prevailing mood was one of euphoria. News of the victory at Leipzig was celebrated with illuminations and a ball at the Guildhall. All the windows of the Infantry Barracks were lighted and the streets crowded. One gentleman's windows were smashed 'for showing lack of candles'. When the Duke of Wellington arrived in Windsor in the first week of August to review his regiment, the Royal Horse Guards, 'His Grace was met at the entrance of the town by a considerable number of inhabitants, some of whom took the horses from his carriage and drew him to the Castle Inn'. Waiting for him in the Guildhall was the Corporation of Windsor who unanimously resolved to present him with the Honorary Freedom of the Corporation. For Christmas, 1814, a Slough butcher, Mr E Shirley, killed an ox for Wellington. Mr Tebbot made some packing cases and Mr Adam of Windsor packed it and sent it to the Duke. In February 1815 Wellington wrote to the Slough butcher to thank him for the beef.

But the rejoicing had been premature. No sooner had the *Express*, which had been recounting all these celebrations, returned to the reporting of more mundane, local issues, than there came 'news of alarming events'. The government of the new French King, Louis XVIII, proved unpopular. Napoleon escaped from Elba, landed near Cannes, and gained the enthusiastic support of the army. News of these events came to Wellington at Vienna, where Napoleon's return at last united the bickering Allies. They now prepared a two-pronged attack on France in the south east, through Alsace and Lorraine and through the Low Countries. Both sides prepared for this final, decisive encounter. Napoleon determined to make his stand in Belgium where the people strongly resented their recent union with Holland. Wellington's army was stationed at Brussels, that of his ally, Blücher (the Prussian General), at Liège. Their object was separately to engage Napoleon, and then unite their forces and march on Paris. At the battle of Waterloo on 18 June 1815 Napoleon was defeated and fled to Paris. Wellington's war dispatch dated Waterloo 19 June informed the government that 'Bonaparte attacked with his whole force the British line supported by a corps of Prussians, which after a long sanguinary conflict terminated in the complete overthrow of the enemy's army'.

Wellington at Waterloo

This official communication did not reach London for some days. In the meantime, according to the *Express* the first and fullest account of the battle was brought by Mr Sutton, a gentleman of Colchester, the proprietor of the passage vessels sailing between that place and Ostend. He was at Ostend when the official news arrived there, and with great zeal and alacrity ordered one of his vessels to sea without waiting for passengers, 'and made the best of his way to town, to relieve the anxiety of government and the public by the earliest information'.

The Allies entered Paris on 3 July where Napoleon surrendered and was sent to St Helena.

For the British, Waterloo was the completion of the Wellington legend. Ironically the battle plan was one of Wellington's least well conceived. 'It was a damned near thing,' he admitted (and it was). Privately he wrote that he 'never was in so hard a fought battle', and that he 'never was forced to exert himself so much'. But the battle of Waterloo entered the public imagination like no other. One of the Duke's staff (quoted in the *Express*) said:

> The Duke has again saved Europe; he was himself everywhere. When the French Cavalry charged, he placed himself in the hollow squares of our Infantry, and when the Cavalry, failing in its efforts to break us, passed by, then he (the duke), charged at the head of his Infantry.

In Windsor, celebrations began all over again with a ball at the Guildhall and prayers of thanksgiving for the late victory, which were read in all the churches. But this time the celebrations were prolonged and repeated annually on the anniversary of the battle. Later, the magnificent new Hall in Windsor Castle would be named 'The Waterloo Chamber', in honour of the victory, and on the first anniversary of the battle, in 1816, officers of the Royal Horse Guards dined with the Duke of York, and 600 soldiers were entertained in the Long Walk with roast beef, mutton, veal, ham and meat pies, wine and ale. Even to this day the Garter Service is held on the most convenient day nearest to the anniversary of Waterloo.

Wellington went on to become Prime Minister (January 1828 to November 1830) but his reactionary and anti-Liberal foreign policy and total opposition to any reform at home, lost him, for a time, much of his popularity. But it was for his prowess on the battlefield that he would ultimately be remembered, and when he died in 1852, he was accorded a State Funeral and buried alongside Nelson, that other famous opponent of Napoleon, in St Paul's Cathedral. Napoleon spent the rest of his life, closely guarded, on St Helena, until his death in 1821.The Express returned from time to time to consider his imprisonment and gave full coverage to his death. (SM)

The Anglo American War

By 1812 Great Britain and her allies had been engaged in the fight against post-revolutionary France and Napoleon for many years. The issues that precipitated the American War had been in existence for some time, and were primarily the restriction of American trade, the impressment of American seamen and insult to their national honour, to which can be added America's desire to expand its borders. By 1811, President Madison began to prepare for war; he realised that Britain was not going to negotiate while she was still fighting in Europe.

While *Foreign Intelligence* includes news reports from America throughout the length of the war, in 1812 Charles Knight is keeping a watchful eye on the American issue and hoping for a peaceful settlement. His main concerns at this time are with matters at home and in Europe, and it isn't until September that Knight starts to examine, as reasonably as he can, the actions that have led to war with America. Writing at length about impressment, he points out that British subjects (which includes the Irish) are by law still British subjects even if they have been given American citizenship. Knight is also at pains to point out the large amount of commonality between the two nations, irrespective of the past, 'the similarity of language, names, and appearance', but also in commerce, where 'not an axe fell in the woods in America which did not put in motion, some shuttle, or hammer, or wheel in England'. He does not, however, baulk from stating that as 'England is engaged in a war for her very existence', and as America encourages deserters, America is therefore 'the first wrong-doer'. He suggests that American expansionism is taking advantage of the war in Europe, as well as suffering undue influence from 'the cloven foot of French councils'. France, 'an overwhelming and unbounded tyranny', is the real enemy. By January 1813, after American naval successes, they have become 'a contemptible and assuming enemy'. Knight is sure British defeats are the result of 'inadequate preparation, uncontrollable circumstances, and the common chances of war', but points out that 'forbearance to an enemy, is deliberate injustice to its own subjects', suggesting the British Government may have been holding back.

Though the war is reported throughout the intervening months, Knight does not comment again until October 1814 as peace appears to be finally arriving in Europe. He is biting in his condemnation of a government that has failed to act immediately on the American front with Britain's large number of experienced troops and her superior navy, has mishandled the opportunity, and sees calamity ahead. He astutely states that now Britain has beaten Napoleon, we must remember that 'gratitude is a short-lived virtue among governments' and sees America garnering support with some European states. Knight insists that 'America should have been subdued before the assembly of the Congress of Europe'. By the end of 1814, Knight fervently believes that the might of the British military can still win the day; that disputes over possession of the Lakes 'must rather be decided by our naval and military forces across the Atlantic, than by our negotiators at Ghent'.

After the message of the President to Congress at the end of 1814, Knight argues that Britain should listen; *fas est ab hoste doceri**. Like all good journalists, he lectures and advises his government, 'vigour and promptitude are the secrets of all success. The minister of Great Britain should forever remember...to be 'Briareus with his hundred hands and Argus with his hundred eyes'.

Yet on 24 December 1814, the Treaty of Ghent, ending the war, was signed and despatched to America. It was ratified by America in February 1815. For a war that Knight saw as illogical and mis-managed, he was fully aware of its greatest ironies; the main cause was no longer a factor when the first shots were fired, and its most famous battle (of New Orleans) was fought after the peace treaty was signed. (CDS)

* One should learn from one's enemies

The Battle of Lundy's Lane, near Niagara Falls, which took place on 25 July 1814. Painting by Alonzo Chappel

Charities

The Royal Dispensary

In November 1817 the newspaper published a letter in support of establishing a dispensary for the sick poor in Windsor. It was signed 'Monacus' and has the style of many a reader's letter published in the paper concerned with social issues that may have come from the pen of Charles Knight Jr. The writer also might have had some inside knowledge, for within two months a committee had been set up chaired by Earl Harcourt, to discuss the Dispensary. By early January a General Dispensary was established and the editor enthused: 'We know of no charity which is more wanted and which is more likely to be effectual in removing and preventing much human misery'. At the end of February a list of subscribers and donors was published in the paper. The largest sum, £150, came from a private fund, £105 as a donation and £52 10s as an annual subscription. The Royal family were supporters and Charles Knight Sr, who was Mayor, donated two guineas and promised an annual subscription of one guinea. Altogether they raised £717 7s in donations and £379 3s in annual subscriptions, a remarkable result.

The General Dispensary was officially opened in Church Street on Tuesday 10 March 1818. Earl Harcourt was president. One of the first things the committee decided was to offer free smallpox vaccination to the children of Windsor.

The medical staff in 1818, besides the two midwives, consisted of the consulting physician, Dr Stewart of Park Street, three surgeon apothecaries, John O'Reilly, John Chapman and William Rendall, with William Jones as house surgeon dispenser.

Each month the newspaper reported the monthly returns of the Dispensary. Those for January 1819 during a time of a smallpox scare show a high take-up for vaccination. By October 1819 only three people came forward for vaccination and numbers remained low until May 1823, when there was another serious outbreak.

By July 1820 figures also showed lying-in patients. As there were only two of them, it shows that the facility was under-used. But Windsor had a separate lying-in charity and besides, women had their babies at home. During the first five years 8,000 people were treated.

The dispensary as it is in 2012

These are the annual figures for 1822:

Patients cured	- - -	745
Partially Relieved	- - -	36
Lying-In, paying 7s. each	-	20
Vaccinated	- - -	59
Discharged for improper Conduct	-	5
Dead -	- - - -	25
	Total	**890**

The total number admitted from the opening of the Institution on the 4th of March, 1818, to the 31st of December, 1822, amounts to 7123; of whom 262 remain under Cure.

Abstract of the TREASURER's ACCOUNTS, from the 1st January, 1822, to the 31st December, 1822.

RECEIPTS.

		£. s. d.
By Balance, 1821 - - - -	-	161 15 3
By Half-year's Dividend on £1150, due Jan. 5.	-	17 5 0
By Ditto on £1300, due July 5 -	-	19 10 0
By Arrears of Subscriptions for 1821	-	3 3 0
By Donation - - -	-	2 2 0
By Subscriptions, 1822 - -	-	463 10 6
	Total	**£ 667 5 9**
Expended - - - -	-	- 657 0 1
Balance - - -	-	- £10 5 8

The Dispensary was mainly an outpatients facility, but there were some care beds. In September 1824 a man working in the Castle fell off the scaffolding and broke his leg. He was taken to the Dispensary. Another casualty of the Castle restorations was 15 year-old William Watts, who was severely hurt in an explosion while pouring molten lead into a hole. He was immediately sent to the Dispensary but lost an eye.

In April 1821 George IV became patron, making it the Royal Dispensary. He made a donation of £25 to the Dispensary and £25 to the lying-in charity, as well as other local causes. Other benefactors left generous legacies; William Grace of Peascod Street left £100 in October 1823 and Mrs De Luc left £25 in July 1824. Mrs Lockman, a benefactor who regularly gave £300 annually to the poor of Windsor, left £100 in her will to the Dispensary and £25 to the lying-in charity in July 1828.

Donors and subscribers to the Dispensary received tickets which they could give to their servants or staff, but the Windsor Dispensary treated anyone, even without tickets. This they particularly emphasised when they called on the poor to be vaccinated free 'without ticket'.

In April 1826 in another letter to the editor signed 'Chirugus' the writer said: 'No paupers are sent out of the parish to the lowest bidder. They are tended at the Dispensary by Sir John Chapman, who is liberally paid for this'.

Poverty and the Poor

From copies of the *Windsor and Eton Express* it is obvious that the problem of caring for the poor was ever to the forefront of people's concerns. In November 1816 the newspaper reported that there were 3,000 men, women and children of the poor and working classes living in Windsor and Clewer, '1,600 of whom stand in immediate need of assistance'. This means that over 50% of the population of Windsor and Clewer were classed as poor or paupers. The poor rate remained at one shilling in the pound from 1818 to 1835 and provided a monthly revenue of between £540 and £590.

The overseers of the poor were responsible for dividing the poor rates among those they decided were most needy. Only the old and infirm, and the most desperate lived in Workhouses, Poor Houses or Alms Houses, others lived in the community; those in need appealed to the overseer for relief. They were called the 'out poor'. All this changed with the Poor Law Amendment Act of 1834 and the introduction of the Union Workhouses, which were to take all paupers.

The Poor Law system had grown out of the problems caused in the past by the ending of the Feudal System where the poor were largely the responsibility of their masters, and the dissolution of the monasteries where food and lodging were given on a temporary basis to beggars and tramps. Over the years it had become obvious that it was necessary to set-up a system of caring and offering help to those unable to provide for themselves. Each parish was made responsible for raising the money through a poor rate and managing their own poor so Windsor and Clewer each built a small workhouse and appointed overseers to manage those applying for relief.

The Windsor Workhouse was endowed in Sheet Street next to the Infantry Barracks in the early eighteenth century with £1000 left in the wills of Richard Topham and his sister Arabella Reeve. It was originally built as a pest-house but as fears of the plague receded it became a workhouse with the proviso that it would revert to its original purpose if necessary. Although Mr Topham and Mrs Reeve donated the money, the running costs and upkeep were the responsibility of the ratepayers of the parish. They put out advertisements each year for managers of the workhouse, like this one of February 1815: 'Datchet poor to let. Wanted a person to contract for the maintenance of the poor of the parish of Datchet for one year'.

When Charles Knight Jr became overseer of the poor in 1818, he suggested visiting the poor in their homes. No one had actually done this before. He recalled in his book *Passages of a Working Life:*

> After a few months' experience of paupers and pauperism I ventured upon a startling proposal to my brother officers – that we should visit the Out Poor in their own homes.
> Never had such an innovation been heard of. Even the paid assistant overseer knew nothing of the real conditions of the 150 recipients of weekly relief. I am afraid the vicar and curate knew as little. The duty of the parish priest was then considered to be fulfilled when he preached to the poor – when he baptized them, married them and buried them.
> Some of our local administrators held that there was personal danger in visiting the poor. Small pox and scarlet fever was ever in our courts and alleys. We did make our visits. We were not always welcome. We discovered some imposture and we saw some real miseries of which we had not been quite aware. The great source of suffering was the want of profitable employment, and for this we had no remedy but the old one of putting the men to work in the parish gravel pit.
> To the assistant overseer squalid filth was the test of destitution, and whining gratitude the test of the deserving poor.

Knight claimed that there were only 150 'out poor' on the books of the overseers in 1818, whereas 1600 had been in desperate need of help in 1816. In February 1823, during a spell of very cold weather, 2,300 Windsor poor were given soup and bread and 600 families were supplied with bushels of coal. There is no explanation for these discrepancies.

It is clear that there was never enough money from the poor rates to cope with the demands of the poor, especially in times of cruel weather or bad harvests like in 1816 or after floods or fires, therefore wealthier citizens were asked for contributions. In November of that year parish officers called for a subscription list to be opened to raise money for 'bread, flour, coals, meat, herrings and potatoes to be made or offered to the poor of Windsor and Clewer, at reduced prices'. The royal family made their usual generous donations and £460 was collected in the first week; Mr Knight Jr was on the committee. In December 1817 soup made of beef, barley, peas and onions was delivered daily to the 'deserving poor' at ½d a quart.

The plight of one poor family was illustrated in the newspaper in May 1816 with a short report about two small children who 'being left asleep in a house in Clewer Lane were severely bitten on their hands and faces by rats'.

Articles on the distressed state of the poor appeared regularly in the newspaper; the lack of employment was seen as the root cause. One reader suggested the poor could be employed picking berries from the whitethorn bushes, which 'could be sold for 6d a bushel' (November 1816), another thought that paupers could be employed in weeding couch grass from farm land, or sweeping the streets, this could earn them 9d to 1s day (December 1816). More practically, as previously instanced in August 1817 Princesses Augusta and Elizabeth bought a machine for dividing hemp and flax in order to provided work for 90 poor of Old Windsor. In December 1817 they visited a factory set up by their direction, where '40 poor men, women and children, who would otherwise have required parochial assistance' were spinning flax.

The 'deserving poor' always seemed to be at the forefront of local concerns. But what about the poor who were 'not deserving'? A report of the overseers of the poor for Windsor in March 1821 stressed that 'the idle and systematic vagrants' and 'persons of profligate and disorderly habits, who beg from place to place' have no right to poor relief which 'is the property of the lame, the blind, the aged, and the infirm'. Itinerant paupers could appeal for a ticket to get some food and a bed for a night in the Poor House, but then had to leave the parish, as only local poor could be supported.

> Benevolent persons are requested to assist this plan by employing the money usually given to vagrants in the purchase of these tickets and to withhold every other kind of assistance except in case of the most evident distress. (March 1821)

In 1827 almost seven million pounds was levied in England and Wales for the relief of the poor (May 1817), and discussions were held around the country about amending the Poor Law

The Poor Law System was obviously flawed and in need of reform as shown by the increasing debate on whether responsibility for the poor should move from the parish to a national system and in 1834 this is what happened with the Poor Law Amendment Act which grouped parishes into Unions and large workhouses were built. The local one was at Old Windsor on Crimp Hill, and out-relief was to be stopped although this was never completely achieved. The poor had to go into the workhouse and men, women and children were separated. This is the workhouse system of Charles Dickens' *Oliver Twist*, a much harsher regime than under the old poor law. (BEM)

Charities

Windsor prided itself on its charitable institutions and generosity in giving to the poor, but there was a qualification, the poor had to be of the deserving kind, no vagrants, vagabonds, beggars or ragamuffins were considered for charity.

In 1812 Windsor had two charity schools, the Free School and the Lady's School (there were other charity schools in Clewer, Eton and Old Windsor), a Lady's Charity for lying-in women, a charity for Promoting Christian Knowledge, a Bible Society, a Society for Apprenticing Children, a Society for Rewarding Diligent Servants, and the Reeve's Alms House. There was also a privately endowed Poor House or Work-house and a small Alms House, these were either side of the Infantry Barracks in Sheet Street. A general statement of the lying-in charity published in the newspaper in January 1824 states that 1071 women had been helped since its opening in 1801.

The Dispensary of 1817 was a major new addition to charitable institutions in Windsor and of the greatest benefit to the poor. The initial subscription list contained 86 names of people who committed themselves to annual subscriptions, as well as giving generous donations. £717 7s was collected in the first weeks, with £379 3s in annual subscription. Another of the important charities set up during this time was the National School, which received generous donations and was of major importance to the children of Windsor.

Charities relied on gifts from wealthy benefactors of the town and neighbourhood. Windsor did not seem to have had a shortage of them; in addition it had the good fortune of Royal patronage. George IV, whatever his shortcomings, was a generous giver, and so were the Royal princesses. Subscription lists for any cause, were always headed with a hefty donation from the royal family. But the less well off, even the soldiers in the barracks, dug into their pockets to give, even just a few pennies, and their names were printed in the *Express*.

Sometimes money was raised to celebrate special events, so that the poorer citizens of Windsor could join in. For the peace celebrations in July 1814 money was collected to provide a dinner for the 'industrious poor'. A long list of subscribers was published in the newspaper. The Duke of York gave ten guineas, the Dean and Canons of Windsor twenty and Charles Knight one guinea.

Money was raised not just for the poor. In June 1813 a subscription list was opened to help a formerly affluent widow 'who is suffering under extreme distress'. An astonishing act of generosity was extended to a local farmer who had fallen on hard times. A meeting of his friends was held at the Swan Inn in December 1814 'to adopt some Plan for extricating him from his present Difficulties'. A subscription soon raised £ 272 17s, Sir Charles Palmer giving £20 and Lord Grenville £30.

Neither was fundraising restricted to local needs. In January 1813 a collection for the 'Russian Sufferers' raised nearly £220 in the first week, in February 1814 money was collected in Windsor 'for the relief of the distress in Germany' caused by the war and in May that year a subscription list was started to help prisoners returning from France who were 'destitute of every necessary'. National causes were also attended to; in February 1827 the newspaper reported that a collection for the relief of distressed manufacturers had reached £234 13s 1d. Princess Augusta gave £10, the Windsor Corporation £20, even the soldiers of the Royal Horse Guards raised £25 8s 9½d out of their meagre pay.

Individual benefactors were often very generous. Mrs Phoebe Thomas set up her own charity, which paid £10 a year to ten poor widows, who must be Church of England and over 50; 'apply in person at the Guildhall by 5 April' (March 1826). Mrs Dawson of St Leonard's Road gave five cauldrons of coal to the poor of Clewer and Windsor in January 1829. Others left money in their wills; Dr James Mingay left £800 to the Charity School of Windsor (February 1813), and Mrs Lockman, who regularly gave £300 annually to the poor of Windsor left £100 each to the Dispensary and the National School, and £25 to the Lying-in Charity (June 1828).

The Price of Bread

Bread was the staple food of the poor and working classes, and the price of bread governed their lives. Bread riots were common when the price was high. Charles Knight Jr describes one such riot when he was a small boy, and the newspaper reported one in Windsor in October 1816. The Mayor had to read the Riot Act outside a baker's shop in the High Street because the baker had been trying to sell loaves for 14½d when the going rate was 13d.

Bread was sold in quartern loaves, which means it was made with ¼ stone of flour and should weigh 4lb. A loaf of bread cost about 5d before the wars with France, but in 1812, when the paper breezed into life, the price had gone up to a record high of 20d. After a good harvest that year, prices steadily dropped to 17d, then 15d and in July 1814 to 11d. During 1816, the year without a summer, prices went up again to 17½d, and to 18½d the following spring. The lowest bread prices during this period were in December 1822, when a quartern loaf cost 6d.

High bread prices were not the only concerns of the people, short measures and adulterated bread was another. In April 1817 a Windsor baker was fined £7 13s 3d for selling bread to the poor 'short of weight'; another had 21 loaves confiscated as being deficient. The loaves were then given to the poor. Adulterated bread was a more serious concern. Bakers used potato mash, pearl ash, even sand to add weight and alum or 'calcined powder' to make it whiter. White bread was the fashion. In January 1818 a quantity of alum was seized from a baker at Walton-on-Thames because he had used it to make his bread whiter, and in May 1818 magistrates warned bakers against the use of 'alum, pearl-ash and potato mash in bread'. This of course added to the health hazards of the poor, as their main source of nourishment was bread.

On the lighter side, an article in the *Express* in October 1817 described beer as 'liquid bread', to persuade people away from drinking gin: 'Good house-brewed beer is wholesome and much healthier than spirits'.

Law and Order

Duelling

Duelling has a long history as a way of settling matters of 'honour' between two men, the combatants usually from the gentry or military, the 'honour' often involving women. In early times duels were fought with swords, but by the nineteenth century pistols were the usual weapon of choice. Each combatant appointed a 'second', a supporter who ensured that proper procedures were followed and arranged for medical assistance if needed. Duels were frowned on by the authorities, with the duellists liable to be arrested and fights stopped by magistrates; if one of them was killed the victor could be prosecuted for murder and hanged. But duellists sometimes felt that if they had met their adversary, honour was satisfied and they fired into the air, which ended the affair.

Duels were regularly reported in the *Express*. The first, in the issue for 5 September 1812, recorded a duel on Bagshot Heath between a Major Jane and a Mr Forman 'in consequence of a dispute about a lady, at Egham race ball'. Both men fired twice but no one was hurt and their seconds 'adjusted the matter' to satisfy both. Two young men called Fenshaw and Hartinger duelled at Ascot Heath race-course in September 1820 'over a female relative'. On this occasion after two 'fires' the parties refused a conciliation and fired again: this time both men were wounded, Hartinger seriously. But in a duel in Kensington Gardens between the Dukes of Buckingham and Bedford over some perceived insult by the Duke of Bedford (4 May 1822), the latter brought it to an end by firing in the air and declaring that his fellow duke was 'the last person' he wished to quarrel with. The Duke of Buckingham accepting a semi-apology, the adversaries shook hands.

Duels could be reported from much further afield: in September 1819 the paper recorded an encounter on Table Mountain in the Cape of Good Hope between a Captain Hussey and a Lieutenant Osborn, which resulted in Osborn's death. Callously the seconds propped the body up against a tree then left, dropping an anonymous note in one of the other officer's rooms. What consequences followed is not recorded.

Political figures were involved on several occasions. In September 1815 there was an aborted duel between Robert Peel, later Prime Minister but then Chief Secretary for Ireland, and the Irish patriot Daniel O'Connell, nicknamed the 'Liberator'. O'Connell's nickname for Peel was 'Orange', for his Protestantism and hostility to Catholic advancement. O'Connell had already killed a man in a duel earlier that year, but in the event the meeting was prevented by magistrates. The antagonists planned to rearrange it for abroad, but in 1817 an encounter at Ostend was called off.

A duel which likewise involved a public figure was reported on 15 May 1824 (in the same issue which gave news of the death of Lord Byron at Messalonghi). It was between Robert Stewart, 3rd Marquis of Londonderry and Colonel of the 10th Hussars, and Cornet Battier likewise of the Hussars who had issued the challenge over what he deemed 'offensive language' against the officers of that corps. The Marquis thought it his 'military duty' to respond. He, a politician as well as a career soldier, had inherited his title after the suicide of his half-brother, another Robert Stewart better known as Lord Castlereagh. (Castlereagh had himself fought a duel with his political rival George Canning in 1809, in which Canning had been injured but Castlereagh only lost a coat button.) Neither man suffered physically from the 1824 encounter, but as reported a week later by the Express the Marquis was severely reprimanded by the Horse Guards for accepting a challenge from a man of lower rank, and Battier was dismissed. The paper also said that the King was severely displeased because such disparity would 'tend to subvert all discipline and subordination'; he declared that 'it mustn't happen again'.

In June 1827 a duel was reported between Sir Jacob Astley and Captain Thomas Garth at Osterley Park. Garth was the illegitimate son of Princess Sophia and his father had been Equerry to George III (see article on the royal family). Astley had brought an action for what was called 'criminal conversation' (ie adultery) between Garth and his wife Georgiana two years earlier when she eloped with Garth, leaving her two children as well as her husband. He now demanded the 'satisfaction in the field which his wounded honour entitled him to demand'. Garth received his shot uninjured, but refused to return fire. While their seconds debated the issue police-officers arrived and Garth was arrested though Astley escaped.

The King would have known and disapproved of this meeting but how did he feel about a duel with potentially disastrous consequences. It was fought 'in the greatest secrecy' between his Prime Minister the Duke of Wellington and Lord Winchilsea on 21 March 1829. This was a time when Wellington was trying to achieve Catholic emancipation against great popular prejudice (the King would rant at him for hours on the subject), but he was also involved in the setting up of the Anglican university, King's College London. To Winchilsea these actions were inconsistent: he wrote a public letter condemning Wellington for acting out of devious motives (and referring with prophetic inaccuracy to 'this sham college, which never will be built'). Wellington felt obliged to respond to the slur and they met at 8am at Battersea (then not much more than boggy ground). A physician stood by in case of the worst. The ground was measured out (12 paces), the pistols were examined, the men took their stations and the order was given 'Fire!' Wellington discharged his pistol and 'struck the lapel of Lord Winchilsea's coat on the left side'. Then Winchilsea fired in the air and the duel was abandoned. The *Express* commented: 'Was it necessary that his Grace ... should peril his life?'

The Duke of Wellington's duel with the Earl of Winchilsea at Battersea fields – 19th century print in the foyer of Wellington Hall.

© King's College London Archives

As a footnote it is worth recording the claim that the last fatal duel in England was fought on the Beaumont estate on Priest Hill between Old Windsor and Englefield Green in October 1852. The adversaries were two French refugees: a former naval captain Frederic Constant and a civil engineer Emmanuel Barthelmey. Constant was fatally wounded. The landlord of the Bells of Ouseley sent word to the police, and Barthelmey was arrested at Waterloo. He was arraigned for murder, though the charge was later reduced to manslaughter. (HD)

Unrest, Insurrection and Riots

The years after the wars with France were marked by an increase of riots and insurrections around the country, both economic and political. They were sparked by chronic unemployment and high food prices exacerbated by the Corn Laws, and by the lack of representation in Parliament of the emerging industrial towns.

Riots were first mentioned in the newspaper in March 1815; during the Corn Bill disturbances two detachments of the Royal Horse Guards stationed in Windsor were called upon to quell riots in London. The following week the newspaper reported the 'alarming events' from France and the return of Napoleon.

When the Horse Guards were again suddenly summoned to London in May 1819 the paper reported that 'the removal of troops produced appalling conjectures', until it became known that they had received the Persian Ambassador.

However, regular reports of riots from around the country were now a feature of the newspaper. They were mainly about improving working conditions and pay, but also an expression of fear about losing out against machines. In Suffolk and Norfolk 'the lower order broke out into open and general disturbance', by breaking machinery and burning farms in May 1816. Unrest among Manchester spinners in 1818 and 1820 turned into open revolt; in 1824 Manchester workers in the silk trade rioted when asked to work an extra hour that is 12 hours a day. Power loom workers rioted in Glasgow in September 1821 and 1823 about forming combinations (unions).

Charles Knight examined the reasons for radical agitation which had begun after the war, in his column *Political Enquirer* in November 1819. In his opinion the 'masses' were poisoned by cheap tracts like those written by William Cobbet: 'Cheap publications [are] almost exclusively directed to the united object of inspiring hatred of the Government, and contempt of the religious institutions of the country'. Knight did sympathise with the poor and the oppressed, but saw their only way out through education. He concluded 'Our object in this Inquiry has been to shew, that we have created an appetite for knowledge and have not provided healthful food'.

Reform agitation reached its crescendo during 1829. In July a radical reformers 'meeting at the Mechanics Institute was fully attended by all ranks, from the 'unwashed artisan' upwards. Henry Hunt was in the chair and Mr Cobbett gave a long speech. Entrance was one penny.

The first great Reform Bill was finally passed in 1832, but it would be many more years before universal manhood suffrage was introduced, let alone the vote given to women.

And finally, the Life Guards were sent from Windsor to quell a riot at Newbury in April 1828, and found the town 'in a state of the most provoking tranquillity, save the ducking of an old woman in a horse pond'.

Crime and the Gaol

Punishment was draconian and prisons foul during the early nineteenth century. Windsor had a gaol built in about 1806, to replace the small prison nicknamed 'coal-house' in the Henry VIII gate. An earlier gaol had been in the old Guildhall on Caste Hill, which was demolished during the early eighteenth century. Charles Knight Jr mentions the new gaol when he wrote about George Street (now station approach):

> There is a whole street of a vicious population where almost every house was a den of infamy. At the bottom of this foul quarter stood our gaol.

Escaped prisoners found ready refuge in George Street; several escapes were reported in the paper. In September 1827, seven prisoners escaped from Windsor gaol, including Charles Dormer, 'a most desperate character', who had only recently returned 'having been ten years at Botany Bay'. He was recaptured in Winkfield several days later; the other six did not get further than Windsor bridge in their distinctive brown and yellow gaol uniforms.

The prison had only two rooms ten feet square and no area for exercise or work. It was used mainly as a holding place before trial, or for drunks to cool off over night. Prison sentences were usually of short duration, maximum one year, more desperate criminals were transported to New South Wales for 6-10 years or life.

Local crime was regularly reported in the press, usually on the last page; the very first issue tells us that 'Thomas Higgs, a post-boy in the employ of the postmaster of this town' was sent to Reading gaol for 14 days hard labour 'for suffering a man of the name of Henry Styles, to ride on the horse with the bag of letters which he was conveying to Staines'. Reports from quarter sessions and assizes from around the country were mostly on page three.

Offenders were arrested by local watchmen and locked up in the gaol until they could be taken before the magistrate in the Guildhall. From 1821 constables were elected to keep the peace, and policemen were first mentioned in the paper in July 1826. Until then the army had been responsible for law and order.

Windsor held its own quarter sessions, but for serious crimes or hanging offences prisoners were sent to the Berkshire sessions or assizes in Reading. Theft of goods over the value of 5s was a potential hanging offence, but even if convicted, rarely carried out.

The second issue of the newspaper carried a report from Newgate prison where eight prisoners had been capitally convicted. Two were ordered to be executed, Catherine Foster for taking a false oath and Joseph Woolman for forgery, the rest, including one highwayman, received the royal pardon from the Prince Regent, and were transported. Six prisoners who were sentenced to death at the Reading assizes in March 1813 were all reprieved.

What was the most common crime during this period? Assault and drunkenness came way ahead of theft and burglary, but were often dismissed with a telling-off, a small fine or a few days cooling off in gaol. Some assaults were more serious: in January 1822 James Bennet and Richard Spoke were sent to gaol for two weeks for assaulting Elizabeth Humphreys, but Thomas Hanslow was held at Windsor gaol to appear at the next session for a more serious assault on Jane Kipplewhite.

Assaults could be verbal. In October 1813 nineteen Datchet villagers were charged with 'the most outrageous and disgraceful conduct'; they had insulted the Reverend J. Philips with cries of 'badger, dog with a white collar'. They had assembled in front of his house with horns and tin kettles, making a noise and shouting 'turn him out, hang him up'. The reason for all this is not clear, the report only said that there was a conspiracy. Nine of the rioters were sentenced to between three and nine months in prison.

Drunkenness was not taken very seriously, although it seems to have been a serious problem; most offenders were discharged with a caution. However, Robert Hammond and James Kleis, 'unfortunate knights of the thimble', and John Harberd, a watchman, were fined 5s each in December 1827 for being drunk in the street early in the morning. And possibly to set an example, Windsor magistrate James Oram was fined 5s for being drunk in the street in April 1827.

Theft of goods worth over 5s and robbery, along with forgery, stealing letters and swearing a false oath were still among a long list of hanging offences; few executions were carried out for theft, but there were several for robbery and forgery. In December 1821, five prisoners were hanged at Newgate, two men for robbery, two women for assaulting men at a house of ill repute, and one 16-year-old youth for passing a forged £10 note.

Theft was always severely punished; some sentences seem today draconian. In March 1813 Thomas James Slaughter, Thomas Green and John Watkins were condemned to hard labour for one year for stealing a bushel of beans; in October 1821 Thomas Manley was publicly whipped and sent to gaol for three months for stealing a handkerchief and assaulting a constable; George Bennet was sentenced to seven years transportation for stealing wood from Frogmore in May 1825; he was sent straight to the hulks at Woolwich from Windsor gaol, for transportation. Charles Jackson was sentenced to be transported for seven years for stealing a sack. (July 1827)

Murder

In February 1817 the body of Mr Longuet, minister of the Catholic Chapel in Reading was found murdered on the Oxford Road. He had been killed with a broad sword and robbed of £13.13s. Soldiers of the Royal Horse Guards, some of whom were stationed in Reading, were accused of the murder, mainly because a sword was used for the murder. The soldiers were found to be innocent, but the paper did not report if the murderer was arrested.

Murders like this were relatively rare, what we find reported regularly is the killing of newborn babies by unmarried mothers. Although there were reports of the death sentence carried out on these women, justice was often very lenient when it could not be proven that the baby was born alive. In March 1817 three women were indicted for the murder of bastard children, May Evans and Sarah Mitchell got two years for concealing the birth of the child, and Amelia, a negro servant born in the West Indies, was acquitted.

Rogues, Vagrants, and Idle Persons

Anyone who did not live in the parish, and who might become liable for poor relief was looked upon as a vagrant and was sent to their own parish or to gaol. Thus Ann Kilminster, 'a very pretty little girl of 17' was brought before the magistrate 'on suspicion of bearing a burthen which might in a few months prove burthensome to the parish'. She had followed a fifer in the barracks. The magistrate told her to either return to her own parish, or marry her soldier.

Others were less kindly treated. Mr Godrey was committed under the new vagrancy act to the treadmill at Reading for three month in January 1825 simply for being a rogue and vagrant, and Hannah Harrington and Ann Eldridge were convicted as vagrants and sent to Reading gaol for two months in November 1826. You could even be sent to gaol on suspicion of intended theft. Thomas Evans was sent to Reading gaol for three months as a rogue and vagabond with 'intent to commit felony'. If you were out of work, workshy or neglected your family you could also find yourself on the wrong side of the law. William Cooper an 'earthenware man' of Clewer, was sent to prison for one month in February 1815 for being an 'idle and disorderly person', spending his money in alehouses rather than maintaining his wife and seven children. In February 1826 William Clarke was convicted as an idle and disorderly person, and for permitting himself to become chargeable to the parish. He was sent to gaol for one month.

Children

Children were not treated any differently from adults during this period, even those as young as 13 were condemned to death. In September 1817, 13 year-old Leary 'sharp and intelligent' with a 'criminal career' stretching back five years, from stealing apples to highway robbery, was charged with stealing a watch. He was sentenced to death, but was later reprieved and transported for life, and 15-year old Thomas Hobbs was sentenced to death for stealing goods above the value of 5s.

In Windsor two boys were sent for trial at the assizes for taking trinkets from the house of leather cutter William Astle; the fact that they were sent to the assizes indicates this was seen as a serious offence. In April 1815 James Johnson and Edward Ewer, 'part of a gang of juveniles' were fined £5 each for breaking the tops of the King's elm trees in the park. As they could not pay the fine, they were sent to Windsor gaol for six months. Even scrumping was a criminal offence: two boys, Samuel Herbert and George Wilkins from Bier Lane, were sent to gaol for two weeks for taking apples from an orchard near the Long Walk, but two small boys who were accused of stealing fencing at the Cavalry Barracks for a bonfire were told off by the magistrate and sent home. (September 1829 and September 1828) One small lad, William Martin, may have been trying to improve himself when he stole two books, but he was thrown into gaol. When his trial finally came up, he was sentenced to one week in custody, having already spent three months in gaol awaiting trial. (May 1829)

However, children were often the victims of crime, but their voices were not heard. In March 1823 the Reverend William Eyre was cleared of raping nine year-old Johanna Quinlan, a girl from the workhouse. He claimed that 'consent was agreed'. The judge summed up: 'was a man to be put on trial for the innocent levity he indulged himself in with children?'

Prostitutes and Homosexuals

Prostitution was not an offence, but prostitutes were arrested for drunken or disorderly behaviour. It was often the only way poor single women could survive, at a time when job opportunities for them were slim indeed. Eighteenth and nineteenth century towns had large numbers of women who survived on the street. Windsor, as a garrison town with two barracks, had the additional quota of camp-followers, as well as women from the surrounding areas, who were attracted by the soldiers. These women often applied for poor relief and the magistrates were always keen to move them on to their own parishes. A woman 'without shoes or stockings and very little else on' asked for relief, in September 1829, but was instead charged with being 'disorderly, abusive and impudent', and threatened with the treadmill if she did not leave the town.

The newspaper called these women 'unfortunates'. In August 1823 eight 'unfortunate women' were apprehended for 'disorderly conduct' and returned to their parishes, in July 1824 six 'unfortunate females of the most abandoned characters' were also sent to Reading house of correction for one month as disorderly persons, and in July 1827 there were eight 'unfortunate females' apprehended in Windsor as vagrants and sent to the house of correction in Reading. This is just a small sample of working girls sent out of town. Then there were the camp-followers. In May 1824 'several young girls who hang around the army in Windsor' were brought before the magistrate; one was sent to gaol in Reading, one 'was owned by a corporal', the rest were sent to their home parishes.

Then there were the local ladies; the most colourful was a Mrs Herbert 'an aged Sybil not less than 70 years of age, but with all the volubility of 17' who was charged in October 1828, with 'inciting children to insult a Mrs Dobson; they both lived in Bier Lane.

Elizabeth Bedborough was mentioned several times. In March 1828 'the notorious Mrs Bedborough' was brought before the magistrate for insulting and assaulting Mr Barrett in the street; she was fined 5s for being drunk and disorderly, and as she could not pay was sent to gaol. A year later she was before the magistrate again for disorderly conduct; she had been seen at night 'passed in and out of the barrack windows'.

She was no relation, as far as we know, of James Bedborough, who had a run in with five 'women of the lowest description', when they moved into one of his unfinished houses, later South Place, and he had to call on the magistrate to get them out in March 1828.

Brothels as we understand them, did not exist, but there were several bawdy houses, where the girls operated from, and often also lived. Most of these were in George Street and were sometimes referred to as brothels. In July 1828 William Churle, 'keeper of a common brothel in George Street' was sent to gaol for one month for assault. William and Lucy Chell, and Henry and Mary Wheeler were fined £50 and £40 respectively, for keeping disorderly houses in George Street in October 1826. During a long case involving bawdy houses and prostitutes in George Street, the Mayor said it was 'a disgrace to the town that such a den of infamy as kept by Mr Haines should be suffered to exist'. Mr Haines was known as 'the one eyed keeper of a notorious brothel, who has lived in Windsor for 76 years'. In October 1829 he was fined £3 for attacking Stephania Winter for non-payment of 4s rent.

A homosexual act was a capital offence, and the paper reported several capital convictions for this 'unnatural crime'. In December 1819 John Markham was executed for an 'unnatural offence' at the Old Bailey. However, a gentleman and a private in the Guards, who were accused of having been seen in the Little Park in the commission of 'the most disgraceful crime that man can be guilty of', were sent to be tried at the quarter sessions, but the charge was eventually thrown out. (October 1824)

Some unusual offences

In March 1813, nine shoemakers were sent to Reading gaol for unlawful combination, (joining a union), to campaign for an increase of wages. William Gutridge had to spend one month in gaol in November 1825 for leaving his work for Mr Goach the coach-maker, unfinished.

In a dispute over toll charges, Lieut. Coffin accused the toll keeper, Edward Cocking, with charging his servant 2d for taking his horse over the bridge while he was on duty. The magistrate fined the toll keeper 40s. (May 1829)

Mr Ferris, a bricklayer's labourer at the Castle accused his wife Mary, 'a little dirty dram drinking old woman', of attacking him with a hammer and a knife, and 'trying to burn down the house'.

Mrs Ferris:...he's used me cruel bad. I've not had a penny of his money....Is it that I've been yer married wife for six and thirty year, the mother of yer leven childer.
Mr Ferris: Oh' 'twould do yer honour good to come and see her, she's drunk as David's sow every night'.

The magistrate pointed out that they had appeared before him some time ago, when the wife had accused the husband of cruelty, and told then 'I think you better try and make it up'. The happy pair left court arm-in-arm! (December 1827)

And finally, Mr Rawlinson, a London magistrate expressed such indignation against an Irishman for having a luxuriant pair of whiskers, that he had him committed not for the assault, but for 'excess of whiskers'. (September 1828).

The Death of Lord Mount Sandford

In June and July of 1828 many columns of the *Express* were taken up with the case of the violent death of Lord Mount Sandford, and its repercussions.

Thursday 5 June was a very busy night in Windsor. The crowds were in an excited state after a day at Ascot races. Just after midnight, there was a fight outside the Castle Inn (now the Castle Hotel). Young Lord Mount Sandford had been to Ascot and was in the Castle Inn having coffee. He heard the commotion, went to see what was going on, was hit and fell into the gutter. Did he bang his head on the kerb or was he injured when he was kicked? There were twenty or thirty people there and everyone who was questioned told a different story about what happened. One thing they did agree on was that cobbler Samuel Brinklett was there and that he administered the blow that made the Lord fall over. The other big talking point was that the Lord was wearing a wig and it fell off and he was found to be bald.

A week later while the injured man still lay in the Castle Inn the newspaper reported on the police court at the Guildhall when Brinklett was accused of also kicking the victim. His arrest was ordered.

Lord Mount Sandford died on the day of the police court, and the following week's paper gave a full report of the inquest which was held at the Guildhall. Mr. O'Reilly, the doctor who attended, gave evidence that he had bled his patient three times and this brought forth letters to the editor of better ways to have dealt with this problem, and considerably damaged the reputation of the surgeon who had several Royal patients. The funeral was held at Windsor Parish Church. The plate on the coffin read

The Right Honourable Henry

LORD MOUNT SANDFORD

Departed this Life June 14th 1828

Aged 23 Years

The Magistrate's Court was at the Guildhall and Samuel Brinklett was named as the murderer and brothers George and Thomas Hunt were named as his accomplices, even though there was very little evidence that either of them were there. This Court was reported in full with many people giving good reports of the three men but they were all sent to Reading Gaol to await a trial at Abingdon.

The judge at Abingdon said that he thought there was no intention to kill and the charge should be manslaughter. Brinklett was very ill-advised when he admitted to the killing. The judge also mentioned the possibility that the treatment given to the patient might very well have been the cause of death. He said that the best advocate for the accused was the prosecuting counsel, but nevertheless the jury found the three men guilty in a joint verdict. The judge gave them the most lenient sentences he could, Brinklett to transportation for life and the two brothers to two years hard labour.

Charles Knight devoted most of the space in his editorial that week to the subject and slated the defence counsels, concluding that if the cobbler had died and the Lord had been accused the verdict would have been very different: '...of the twenty or thirty persons present—gentlemen and cobblers—one was about as guilty as another.' (PM)

Life and Death

Smallpox

The speckled monster, as smallpox was often called, was a common disease during the nineteenth century. It led to disfigurement, blindness and often death and was greatly feared. Inoculation with smallpox matter had been introduced during the eighteenth century and was widely used, often by wise women and quacks. It had one draw-back: the patient could infect others during the incubation period or develop full blown smallpox and die.

Jenner's vaccination with cowpox matter was not so easy to administer and had to be done by a doctor, but people were reluctant to try it.

Prince Frederick, Duke of York (1763-1827) was very impressed with Jenner's trials and introduced compulsory vaccination in the British Army in 1811 to great effect, but persuading the general public to come forward to be vaccinated was more difficult.

Articles in the newspaper reflected the ongoing struggle to get people vaccinated. The benefits of the new vaccine were discussed in an article on 15 August 1812, in which it was claimed that mortality had dropped in London areas where vaccination was adopted.

In Windsor a meeting of Friends of vaccination, headed by Arthur Vansittart, aimed to remove the prejudice of the poor, and set up a subscription list to provide free vaccination for them (25 June and 16 July 1815).

The Cow Pock, early 1800s by H. Humphrey

The new dispensary regularly urged the poor to come forward, even offering a reward of one shilling to mothers who brought their children to be vaccinated. But only during times of large-scale outbreaks as in 1819, could the dispensary report that in March 145 people and in April 45 people had been vaccinated. Usually their monthly returns were in single figures.

Sadly during an outbreak in 1823 in Datchet Lane, a four-year-old child died after her mother had inoculated her with smallpox matter from a neighbouring child.

It is difficult to understand why the poor were so reluctant to get free vaccination, but rather paid up to 2s 6d to get a 'wise woman' to inoculate their children. In November 1827 several children died in Windsor during another outbreak, after being inoculated. The newspaper lamented:

> It is extraordinary that people should be so thoughtless as to trust the lives of their children to an ignorant woman when many respectable surgeons are ready to vaccinate them gratis.

The problem was not tackled until the government brought in the Vaccination Act following the epidemic of 1838 which made inoculations illegal. During that year Berkshire had 1,670 cases of smallpox with 288 deaths.

Medications and Medical treatment

There was hardly a front page of the *Express* that did not have an advertisement for some miracle cure, ointment, salve or pill. A list of medications sold by Charles Knight at the newspaper office first appeared in 1816, with over 90 different items; in 1822 that had increased to 130 items.

Cures for consumption and ointments for the itch, worm powders, and pills for stone and gravel were for sale. 'Widow Welch's female pills' vied with Hooper's female pills; three different types of corn plasters and salves were on offer: was there a problem with ill-fitting shoes? In addition, medication for animals like distemper powder and purging balls for dogs and horses could be bought from Charles Knight, as well as vermin control such as Hampshire Miller's rat powder; even a cure for 'the bite of mad dogs' was available. These would all have to be stored at Knight's Castle Street office, which turned him into a dispenser as well as printer and bookseller.

These 'cures' were advertised individually as well, giving more information about them; Royal Brunswick Corn Plasters 'from an original Recipe belonging to her late Majesty' was available in boxes at 1s 1½d from

The following approved

PATENT MEDICINES

Are kept constantly on Sale by C. KNIGHT & SON
Castle-Street, Windsor:

And may be had of the Newsmen circulating this Paper.

Alsana extract.
Anderson's Scot's pills, prepared by Inglish
Aromatic Vinegar
Butler's tooth powder
Bucknall's ditto
Brodum's nervous cordial and botanical syrup
Betton's British oil
British corn plaister
———— Herb snuff and tobacco
Blondell's specific for the gout
Barrett's ointment for the eyes
Barclay's antibilious pills
Blaine's distemper powder for dogs
———— alterative cleansing powders
———— effective worm medicines
———— ointment for the mange
———— purging balls
———— astringent balls
———— tonic balls
———— ointment for canker
———— effective wash for canker
Collins' cephalic snuff for the head ach
Ching's worm lozenges
Charcoal tooth powder
Cundell's balsam of honey
Court plaister
Chinese vegetable balsam
Dalby's carminative for the bowel disorders
Daffy's elixir, an universal family medicine
Dawson's lozenges
Duchesne's rheumatic tincture
Essence of Tolu
———— of coltsfoot
Friar's balsam, for cuts
Freeman's bathing spirits
Greenough's tooth tincture
———— Tolu lozenges for coughs
Godbold's vegetable balsam
Green's honey lozenges
———— Tooth-ach pills
Gowland's lotion, prepared by Vincent
German corn plaister
Glasse's magnesia
Gould's anti-scorbutic lotion
———— powder
———— Anthritic liniment
———— digestive ointment
———— eye water
———— opening powder
———— pile ointment
Garthshore's antibilious pills
Garratt's aromatic snuff
Huxham's tincture of bark

Hooper's female pills
Hemet's pearl dentrifice
Hill's balsam of honey
Hampshire Miller's rat powder
Hickman's pills
Hudson's bleaching liquid
Hunt's family pills
James' fever powder
———— anpleptic pills
Jones' rheumatic tincture
Jackson's itch ointment
———— asthmatic candy
Issue plaister and pease
Kennedy's corn plaister
Magnesia lozenges
Millman's itch ointment
Manning's tooth powder
Macassar oil
Moore's cancer ointment
Ormskirk medicine for the bite of mad dogs
Oxley's essence of ginger
Peppermint lozenges
Paregoric ditto
Refined liquorice
Radcliff's gout tincture
Steer's opodeldoc, for sprains, &c.
———— oil for convulsions
Salt of lemons
Sicilian bloom, or vegetable flesh powder
Spilsbury's antiscorbutic drops
Stevenson's arcanum for the hair
Spyring and Marsden's pure lemon acid
———— aerated lemonade
———— soda powders
Solomon's balm of Gilead
Solander's English senitive tea
Scot's nankeen dye
———— liquid blue
Tonquin's nervous cordial
Trotter's tooth powder
———— wash for the tooth-ach
Vincent's tooth powder
Vancouver's cement, or iron glue
Widow Welch's female pills
Whitehead's essence of mustard
———— Family cerate
Wheatley's itch ointment
Watson's purging horse balls
———— alternative ditto
———— diuretic ditto
———— cordial ditto
———— mercurial purging ditto
———— blistering ointment
———— distemper balls for dogs
Wooding's embrocation
———— improved guttæ vitæ

'Druggists, Booksellers and Medicine Venders' (December 1820). Haycock's 'infallible remedy (which) excels at curing deafness and noises in the head' was advertised In October 1813; the following year the claim was that Haycock's 'Pectoral Elixir has cured 3,000 of Asthma and consumption' (January 1814). Ching's Patent Worm Lozenges were an 'unparalleled success for worms, fits and pains in the stomach', sold in boxes at 2s 9d each and for the poor in paper at 1s 1½d (April 1815) 'Hayman's Genuine original Maredant's Antiscorbutic Drops' also cured 'scurvy, leprosy, piles, rheumatism, tumours, contracted joints' etc (Sep 1819). Dr Sydenham's family pills of health promised to cure 'head-ache, loss of appetite, lowness of spirit, flatulence' and more.

Barkley's original ointment was advertised with schools and families in mind (October 1818), as '... a safe, speedy and effectual cure of the itch'. It was stressed that this ointment 'does not contain mercury'. Mercury was an ingredient in a number of medications and was regularly used for venereal disease. However, most 'cures' sold by Knight were harmless vegetable concoctions, or based on honey, lemon, peppermint, vinegar or ginger.

Medical practitioners in Windsor were no wiser, although treatment for broken bones and often amputations seem to have been dealt with successfully, perhaps with much experience on battlefields; a nine-year-old girl, daughter of Mr Lintut of Sheet Street, had to have her arm amputated after she was accidentally shot in the elbow. She was said to be recovering well (August 1814). The Duke of York fell as he caught his spur in the loop of his pantaloons and broke his arm when he visited the King in Windsor in April 1819. He was treated by Mr O'Reilly who set his fracture. Daily bulletins about his health stressed that he 'was free from fever'. George Smith, a young man working in the Castle, lost both his legs unloading heavy stones. Mr O'Reilly successfully amputated both his legs. When the King heard about the accident, he sent Smith £20, and promised to pay him one guinea a week for life (January 1827).

There was also a case of trepanning reported in the paper in September 1813. A three-year old boy, son of Mr Luff of Slough was 'run over by a post-chaise and his skull dreadfully fractured'. He was said to be improving after trepanning treatment, by cutting a hole in his skull to relieve the pressure.

But the most common treatment, especially for fevers, was bleeding. The Prince of Wales was so distressed over the death of his daughter that it 'became necessary to bleed him twice besides cupping him' (November

1817). The Duchess of Clarence (later Queen Adelaide) suffered a miscarriage, after which 'it was deemed necessary to bleed her several times'; and the Duke of Kent was bled three times and twice cupped as he lay seriously ill with cold and inflammation of the chest. He died. Queen Caroline was also 'copiously bled' before she died of a 'bowel obstruction', for which she also took 'a large dose of magnesia'. Some survived the treatment, the Rev. Dr Stanier Clarke, private chaplain to the King, 'was seized with a fit of paralysis for which he was copiously bled', and recovered (Jan 1829).

Accidental Deaths

Accidental deaths and injuries from a variety of causes were widely reported in the newspaper, as they are these days. Many of these were due to the proximity of the river, as described elsewhere, but road accidents, fires, poisonings, shootings and workplace accidents also took their toll.

The capricious nature of horses, poor road conditions and the fragile structure of horse-drawn vehicles were the subject of many reports. For instance, in February 1813, a carriage belonging to Mrs Blight overturned in Park Street, injuring three passengers. The horses had bolted and jumped a four foot wall at the entrance to the Long Walk, dragging the carriage with them. In the same week, a lad working for the Maltster Mr Cooper was driving a cart loaded with barley and chaff in Datchet Lane, and slipped off the path into the river which was swollen after rain. The horse and cart were found later at Datchet Bridge, but the lad was still missing. In May that year a carriage accident in Peascod Street left a horse with a broken leg, and in August 1814 a labourer fell from a wagon load of peas, breaking his collarbone, and was 'dangerously ill'.

In just one month in May 1815, there were four accident reports. In Staines, the Southampton mail coach was changing horses at the Red Lion when they bolted and the coach overturned. Three horses were later caught near Egham and one at Chobham. Mr Proudman, a messenger in a gig with dispatches, broke a rein near Frogmore, and as his horse took off he steered it into Datchet Lane. Trying to avoid a dray near to the Royal Oak, he bumped the gig and the wheel shattered. In this instance the rider and horse were unhurt. Mr Tebbott was thrown out of his gig in Park Street, with a wheel passing over his leg after his horse bolted along the Long Walk. The horse finally came to a halt in Sheet Street after smashing the gig against a post. One rider who was less fortunate was a servant working for Messrs

Ramsbottom and Baverstock, who was driving a dray from Windsor to Englefield Green. As the horse took fright, he was thrown between the 'dogs' and the wheel, suffering serious head injuries 'with little hope of recovery.'

A few weeks later a horse fell outside the Crown Inn in Peascod Street, crushing its rider's leg. In May 1817, a carpenter driving a gig in Windsor Great Park smashed into a tree and his wife was killed. In June 1826, the Windsor to London coach was travelling at 7 mph when the axle broke. One passenger tried to leap to safety, but was fatally injured when the coach fell on him. The other eleven passengers were unhurt. Three years later on the same route, a horse drawing the London coach bolted into the turnpike gates at Hounslow, and a female passenger was injured. Pedestrians did not escape unscathed, and amongst other reports was one of an Eton scholar who was knocked down by a cart, and his condition was described as 'precarious.'

Domestic fires were common, and nearly all the fatal accidents involved young children. In many cases, the children had been left unsupervised, and their clothing caught fire when they moved too close to the hearth. In October 1813 John Steel aged three burned to death at Spital and so did Sarah Dyckes aged two in Eton. Also in Eton, Sophia Glazier died in November 1814 while her parents were out, and tragically in November 1821 a paralysed father, George Morgan of Windsor, watched helplessly as his child burned to death in front of the fire. Two more occurred in March 1821 when William Wright aged nine died at Eton College after his nightshirt caught fire and a labourer's four-year-old child died in similar circumstances at Frogmore dairy. October and November 1829 were particularly tragic, with a three-year-old child burned in Clewer Lane, also four-year-old William Green in the Infantry Barracks after being left alone, and four-year-old John Thom whose clothes caught fire in Old Windsor. The coroner was moved to give a warning about the hazards, saying it was his third such inquest in ten days.

Accidental poisonings were occasionally reported. Confusion over medicines sometimes had fatal results as in December 1816 when an infant was killed by arsenic, given in mistake for Godfrey's cordial. In March 1823 a mother poisoned her two daughters with arsenic which she believed to be magnesia, and in August 1825 a London man similarly mistook arsenic for milk of magnesia. Gin was relatively cheap at 9s to 12s per gallon, and was available in many households. In March 1815, the five-year-old son of William Brown of Datchet died after drinking half a pint of it. In February 1827, a William Drabble believed that a 'noggin' of gin would cure his children's worms.

One was 'cured' but two younger children of six and eight died. In September 1828, several children were taken ill after eating deadly nightshade berries, and one of them died. A coachman working for Mr Mont of Forest Farm Winkfield saved himself by riding to Windsor to buy some magnesia after he had mistakenly swallowed oxalic acid instead of Epsom Salts.

Carelessly discharged shotguns were responsible for several non-fatal accidents. In August 1814 in Sheet Street a nine-year-old girl was shot in the arm, which had to be amputated, and a similar accident happened in November 1826 to John Sedding, a baker in Eton. Further afield, at a shooting party in Suffolk in January 1823, the Duke of Wellington accidentally shot his host Lord Viscount Granville's nose and cheeks, and in December 1825 at Lulworth Castle the Duke of Gloucester shot Captain Waldegrave in the eye.

In the days before stringent Health and Safety Regulations, workplace accidents were common. With much building work on the Castle, the Parish Church and Windsor Bridge, there was an increased potential for accidents. In August 1814, scaffolding collapsed in the High Street and three men and a boy were seriously hurt, and in June 1822 James Strebbs, a labourer, lost three fingers while working on Windsor Bridge. He apparently stumbled and steadied himself by grabbing one of the piles just as the 'monkey' or pile-driver came down on his hand. An appeal was made for donations to help to support his wife. In November of that year, the river was particularly treacherous after heavy rain, and the difficulty of negotiating the bridgeworks became apparent after the barge *Prince Regent* smashed into the headland known as the Cobler and was grounded on the Windsor shore. Its cargo of paper and flour was seriously damaged. Only one week earlier, the newspaper had carried a warning on the front page that the water level had risen considerably and barges should proceed with extreme caution or suspend their voyages altogether. In the following Spring, the river was still high when Mr Aldridge, a butcher from Taplow, was returning home from Windsor market by ferry with his horse and cart. The horse jumped overboard, leaving the cart suspended for several minutes, until the butcher was obliged to push the cart as well, losing his horse and his stock.

In September 1824 a Mrs Fenton had her leg amputated after it was crushed by a timber wagon in Datchet Lane, and in April 1825 at the nearby brewery belonging to Messrs Ramsbottom and Legh a long-serving employee died after falling from the cooler into Mr Ramsbottom's garden.

Building works at the Castle were particularly hazardous. In one week in

November 1826, a glazier named Spiers broke his ribs in a fall from a plank and a labourer named Vickers was blinded by lime exploding in his face. Two months later, George Smith lost both legs while moving heavy stones. In February the following year, 15-year-old William Watts lost an eye when molten lead exploded as he poured it into a stone plug hole in the Castle, and one month later a man removing a tree near to the Hundred Steps was half-scalped when it fell on him. One resilient stonemason fell 30 feet from the Duke of York's tower, his fourth serious accident in three years.

Children were vulnerable in the workplace, and in 1826 a 12-year-old boy called Jones was killed at Cookham Paper Mill when his apron got caught in machinery, and 13-year-old Thomas Cottrell was injured when he was dragged into a threshing machine at Cippenham.

The newspaper reported many accidents from further afield. In October 1814 a beer vat exploded in London, spilling 3500 barrels of strong beer, which flooded several streets including cellars. The explosion demolished the brew house and two houses, leaving eight people dead. Even further afield, in Paris, was the curious case of the woman who was found dead after regularly drinking brandy to excess. She was found to be 'much burned in the absence of fire or candles' and the inquest concluded that she had died of 'spontaneous combustion.' (SA)

Rabies

Deaths from rabies, or hydrophobia, were frequently reported in the *Express*. The first mention was in May 1815 when a labourer died at Beaconsfield after a mad dog bit him on the nose. In September 1817 there seem to have been a series of 'outbreaks' of rabies in Portsmouth, Stamford and Doncaster; several people died after being bitten by mad cats and dogs. In August 1821 two men who came to the assistance of a 'charity schoolboy' who was attacked by a mad dog paid with their lives, as did the boy. But a dog, which went on the rampage in Henley in November 1825, was killed after biting several dogs and a pig. All were destroyed. Charles Knight's Newfoundland yard dog was put down after attacking a Labrador, biting a horse and a lamb and killing several ducks and fowl. He was suspected of being rabid (September 1822).

Remedies and cures for hydrophobia were common, but ineffective, although in October 1812 one man with rabies was said to have survived after being bled twice. Among the list of patent medicines sold by Charles Knight and Son in June 1816 was 'Ormskirk medicine for the bite of mad dogs'. The King's stag-hounds were taken to Brighton and washed daily when signs of rabies appeared among them, but this has 'unfortunately proved ineffectual' and the whole pack had to be destroyed. In August 1828 the newspaper printed a recipe for the bite of a mad dog, which hung in Sunninghill Church:

> six ounces of rue picked from the stalk,
> four ounces of garlic,
> four ounces of Venice treacle,
> four ounces of the scrapings of pewter,
> boil in two quarts of strong ale until reduced to one quart.

This could be given to man, dog or applied to the bite, but there is no record if anyone survived the 'cure'.

Disasters at Sea

The *Express* newspaper provided the inhabitants of Windsor with a window onto the wider world. Though news came in slowly, people who may never have travelled far from the land-locked town could learn of events around the globe, including some harrowing tales of sea disasters.

The paper of 22 December 1816 carried details of the loss more than a month before off the coast of Newfoundland of the *Hollander* which had been transporting soldiers, with women and children, from service in Canada back to Deptford. On a stormy night the ship struck rocks just off the shore and quickly began to break up. Many lives were lost in the confusion. The best that could be done was to launch a boat from the stern of the ship with the first mate and a number of seamen, with the aim of making land on a steep promontory nearby, then carrying more across. With difficulty they reached the rocky outcrop and scrambled up, but the boat was wrecked. At this gloomy moment the ship's master had the idea of sending a line across by a dog which was on board:

> The animal was brought aft, and thrown into the sea with a line tied round his middle, and with it he swam towards the rock upon which the mate and seamen were standing: It is impossible to describe the sensations which were excited at seeing this faithful dog struggling with the waves, and, in reaching the rock, dashed back again by the surf into the sea, until at length by his exertions he arrived with the line.

That rope was then used to send across a stronger one, to which slings were attached, enabling many lives to be saved. Next morning at low tide the survivors were able to cross to the mainland and seek human habitation. Thanks to an ingenious captain and a heroic dog 130 from the doomed ship were saved. A new life began as well, when one of the rescued women gave birth on the top of the rock.

Human ingenuity and resilience in face of appalling conditions were also shown by crew and passengers of the *Blenden Hall*, which was wrecked in the South Atlantic in July 1821 while on a journey from London to Bombay. Eight crew members were lost, but everyone else got ashore on Inaccessible Island, part of the Tristan d'Acunha archipeligo, which was as inhospitable as it sounds. It was the southern winter, the survivors had escaped only with what clothes they had on, and it was days before they could light a fire. But they managed to make tents from bales of cloth washed ashore, and an iron buoy cut in half formed a cooking pot. All they had to cook in it, however, was what they could scrounge from the wild: they afterwards claimed to have subsisted mainly on penguins and their eggs. Then, on 8 November:

> The carpenter and three of four of the crew embarked in a small punt [*sic*], made out of the wreck with surgical instruments, which were thrown on shore, and reached Tristan d'Acunha where they procured two whale boats, and brought those that remained on Inaccessible Island away.

Eventually the survivors managed to take ship from the main island, living to tell their extraordinary tale of endurance.

There were a number of shipwrecks reported from around the shores of Britain. In August 1821 the packet-ship *Earl Moira* sailing from Liverpool with over 100 passengers, struck a sandbank off the Cheshire coast. But the Captain, 'inebriated and consequently bewildered', assured passengers there was no danger and that high tide would lift the ship off the sand. He refused to run up a distress signal. But in heavy seas the rising tide flung the vessel broadside and she began to break up. There was panic and several passengers, plus two horses, were swept off the deck to their deaths. Eventually a life-boat and other small craft came to the rescue but many died, including the captain. Another ship loss, in November 1827, was the *Queen Charlotte*, a Leith smack, which was run down by a collier near Lowestoft. The crew had made frantic signals to the collier, but only a young lad was at the helm, and the *Queen Charlotte* was severed in two. Remarkably no lives were lost, but '76 puncheons of superior whiskey' destined for 'gude Scots' in London went down with the ship.

It was brandy that was reponsible for the loss of the *Fame* in July 1824. This ship was carrying home from Bencoolen in Sumatra Sir Stamford Raffles (1781-1826), founder of Singapore, his wife and others. The ship had fortunately not travelled far from land when it was set ablaze by a steward who'd gone down to a store-room, broached a cask of brandy and thereafter set it on fire. Since the ship was carrying powder and salt-petre it was instantly decided to take to the boats. Most left the ship only half-dressed:

> Lady Raffles had on her night clothes, and had not time to put on even a pair of stockings. Most of the people were without hats. They had not time to get a drink of water or any thing to eat; only one boat had a compass.

Nevertheless no lives were lost. What were lost however, were Sir Stamford's priceless collections of plants, fish, animals and birds, along with thousands of natural history drawings and paintings, maps, and his scientific papers, both published and unpublished. Gone forever too were his notes for a planned history of Sumatra, for him a devastating blow.

The hazards of the high seas were not confined to bad weather and human error. Correspondence from Jamaica was quoted on 16 July 1825, announcing the likely loss of the *Lady Wellington* to pirates. She had reputedly been carrying £100,000. These pirates of the Carribean were plunderers who knew that 'Dead men tell no tales': the *Lady Wellington*'s fate was gruesomely revealed when 24 headless bodies were washed up on the shores of Curaçao.

Disasters can occur not only out at sea, but at the margins of the land. A story picked up by the *Express* in May 1817 is a reminder of a tragedy of recent times: that a party of cockle pickers, men, women and children, had been drowned at Lavan Sands, near Bangor in north Wales. This is a fine long stretch of sand and mud-flats with freshwater streams flowing through them, an important site today for wintering waterbirds which feast on the cockles and other marine creatures found there. At low tide the sands are firm, but as the tide comes in they become dangerous. These cockle pickers were a party of twelve 'poor people' seeking the bounty of free food, but they became disorientated when thick fog descended and all were drowned.

When stories such as these were printed Windsorians would have read them with fascinated attention, but no doubt also with thankfulness that they were secure in their homes, not tossing on the ocean or lost on the sea-shore. (HD)

International Events

> It will be the endeavour of the editors
> 1. To collect and arrange political facts and economical facts...obscure and undigested...yet of essential importance to be understood...
> 2. Furnish a weekly summary of political events to form the right judgement in objects of universal importance.

These objectives are stated in the first issue of the *Windsor and Eton Express*, to give the reader an idea of the scope of the new weekly paper and keep him or her up-to-date in a period of cataclysmic events.

International affairs were usually printed on page 2 under headings *Political Inquirer* and *Foreign Intelligence;* occasionally a vital piece of late news was added on page 4 under the heading *Postscript*. Foreign and home sources were used: newspapers, journals, reports, correspondence, dispatches from the various war fronts. Reading news that had first appeared in the *Bulletin of the Grand Army*, *St Petersburgh Gazette,* or *Gottenburgh Mail* gave a sense of immediacy in addition to variety in reportage. These sources were already two months old or more when received in London. Other foreign and provincial newspapers were added later, together with respected journals such as the *Edinburgh Review,* and it was from the *London Gazette* which covered these that the editor culled his news.

By 1812 the Napoleonic Wars had consumed most of the European mainland and the Grand Army threatened Moscow. The Battle of Borodino was fought on 11 September and reported on 10 October 1812. The Russian army retreated east of Moscow leaving the French to brave the oncoming winter weather. Throughout the following weeks the newspaper quoted from *Bulletins of the Grand Army* the French version of events. The *Gothenburg Mail* and *St Petersburgh Gazette* reported the disasters. In *The Political Inquirer* columns the editor discussed 'the military system of Bonaparte' and 'the war in Russia' and requested 'contributions for the relief of the people of Russia'.

The cold weather began on 7 November and it was reported that every night there were losses of horses and men. The temperature dropped to −18° on 17 November and 36,000 horses perished (27 December 1812). The same issue reported the French forces retreating, with Napoleon speeding ahead to reach Paris, quoting the *London Gazette Extra* which published dispatches from St Petersburgh to the Foreign Office in London.

In the Iberian Peninsular the French army in Spain had been defeated at Salamanka [*sic*: later the paper used the modern, anglicised spelling of Salamanca] and the Duke of Wellington's dispatches were printed. Details of the battle and casualty lists were published on 22 August.

Across the Atlantic the United States Congress had declared war against Britain and in the first edition there was a list of grievances and reports from Boston of flags flying at half-mast in dismay at the effect on trade. There were fears of an invasion of Canada and Nova Scotia.

Naval battles were reported under the heading *Naval Intelligence*, giving many instances of the Royal Navy's 'Stop and Search' of enemy ships and foreign slavers.

Newspaper coverage of the French wars was substantial up to and including the Congress of Vienna in 1818. Alliances of the Allies, the Battle of Leipzig in 1813, Napoleon's exile to Elba and subsequent escape, Louis XVIII's triumphant return to France, the 'Hundred Days' and finally the Battle of Waterloo were all reported with information taken from the *Times*, *London Gazette*, *Journal des Débats* and reports to Parliament from commanders including Wellington. After June 1815 the paper reported 'Glorious victories in the Netherlands' and quoted Wellington's dispatches.

Negotiations for peace, the treaties and their implications for Britain were reported (22 November 1818), detailing the Acts of the Congress in Vienna, which had been signed on 15 November. With peace in Europe communications became faster. Britain retained Malta and St Lucia and was awarded Ceylon, formerly part of the Dutch East Indies. Boundaries were fixed between the United States and Canada, and in Europe a 'status quo' was arranged, with a few changes. Exchanges and the return of prisoners were reported.

This settlement of affairs might have relegated French news to minimum coverage but Napoleon was still of interest to readers. His exile on St Helena with occasional reports on his health, interests and accommodation appeared, with mention of 'harsh treatment' on 23 August 1818. Napoleon's death on 5 May 1821 was reported (1 July), with a description of the lying-in-state, and burial on the island. There was comment on his 'heroic death' (he had been ill for 6 weeks) in the next issue, supplied by the Naval Office of St Helena. News of Napoleon's death was overshadowed by home news of Queen Caroline, her behaviour at the Coronation, followed by her death and funeral arrangements (see article on the Royal Family).

After the Peace Treaties, international news coverage continued to inform the reader about events in Europe, the Americas and the Far East. Spanish and Portuguese colonies in South America revolted and gained independence, some European rulers overthrew the countries' new Constitutions and repressed rebellions, as in Spain and Naples. Greece struggled for independence from Turkey, drawing support from major European powers. Britain remained neutral and pursued trading links overseas, but was apprehensive of unrest spreading amongst workers at home.

Readers of the *Express* were aware by now of England's place in an enlarged world, her navy protecting trade, ships transporting emigrants and convicts to newly-discovered territories that could be opened up for agriculture, mining and other benefits. An excerpt was printed from the *Literary Chronicle* on population (7 October 1821). Drawing on the 3rd population census and estimates it concluded that Britain had a population of 70,000,000 and compared this with the Roman Empire of 120,000,000, but most of them were slaves. The paper concluded proudly:

> In short ... the British Empire in power and strength and value may be stated as the greatest that ever existed on earth.

The Windsor reader could contemplate this statement as he studied the pages of his weekly newspaper, and wonder at the improved speed with which news arrived. In January 1816 there was a report of a vessel arriving from Australia after a journey of less than five months! In 1818 news was given of the discovery of Bathurst, Lachlan and McQuarrie rivers in New South Wales, and the possibility of opening up land for agriculture. An article from the *Edinburgh Review* (6 September 1818) comments on *Birkbeck's Notices* on America which gave information to emigrants intending to farm. Later that month emigration from Bristol to America of miners from Abergavenny was noted, followed by news of 300 emigrants to Montreal from western Scotland, the first of 1,000 artisans whose passage was paid by the government.

Voyages of discovery were reported, new lands discovered by expeditions searching for new routes. There was a polar exploration of arctic regions (18 October 1818) and from a Hull paper the discovery of the esquimaux by an expedition to the north-west Atlantic.

Reports and letters from Missionary Societies provided information not only on progress in distributing Bibles and tracts, and translating these into Eastern languages, but also their views of the customs and culture of the 'heathen'. The Newberry Bible Society grandly aimed to 'civilise the barbarians, enlighten the ignorant, rationalise superstition' (30 August 1818), while the British and Foreign Bible Society marked its 16th anniversary in 1820 and reported that the 'Calcutta Bible Society covers China where Bibles were not allowed to be imported, and the South Seas'. A Dr Morrison was translating the Bible into Chinese, and the Rev. W Ward, a missionary, described the condition of Indian women as 'illiterate, without education, cultivation' and discussed the prevalence of child marriage and suti (the burning of widows on their husband's pyres).

India was 'the bright jewel of the British Empire which Bonaparte had so enviously wished to deprive us of', and one of the dangers of Napoleon's incursion into Egypt was the threat to India ,where the East India Company had extended its reach, power and trade. The Elizabethan Charter which gave the Company trading monopoly came up for renewal in 1813: plans to open Far East trade to other London merchants and seaports were strongly resisted. Correspondence between the Company and the British government were reported, together with a history of the India trade in January issues.

By 1813 British influence extended throughout north and central India, successfully promoted by Wellington's brother, Viceroy Lord Wellesley, 'the uncompromising empire-builder'. Dispatches and other communications reached London at least six months in arrears so that news of the Maratha Wars in March 1818 did not appear until 27 September. News from India kept the Windsor reader informed not only of wars, but military sweeps against marauding bands (the Pindari, 1817), native rulers' attacks on Company strongholds (Travancore 1812, Pune 1817), but of the life of Company servants. A 'Lion hunt near Bombay', in October 1813, provided a thrilling account of adventures.

Its Charter renewed, East India Company news was regularly reported, alongside news sent by missionaries, as trade and influence expanded into the East Indies and China, but by 1830 commercial ambition and strategic paranoia sensed danger from a Russian invasion over the Himalayas. From henceforth it would not be the French but the Russians who were the potential enemy, culminating in the Crimean War in the 1850s.

The reporting of international events provided an informal education. Charles Knight's newspaper expanded horizons, encompassing wartime events in the early years of publication and matters of world-wide interest by the time he sold up and left for London in 1827. (SS)

National Events

National news was reported mainly on the two middle pages (2 and 3), with small news items included under the heading *Miscellaneous*. Frequently, provincial and local newspapers were quoted, such as the *Leeds Mercury* or *Maidstone Gazette*. Major issues of the day – the Corn Laws, Free Trade, Parliamentary Representation, Civil Unrest, Catholic Emancipation, were examined and presented to form 'the right judgement'. The shadow of the French Revolution and Wars was never far away, extending well into the 1820s. The change to a peace-time economy, fears of Jacobinism with the activities of Radicals, underlay most of the news content. The editors kept an impartial view, presenting facts taken from their main sources, and keeping within the constraints of the law.

Ireland, nearer to home but of equal strategic and political importance became a frequent topic in the newspaper. As back-door to the mainland and vulnerable to foreign invasion it was regarded with apprehension especially during the Napoleonic Wars. A 'foreign' religion – Catholicism – and ideas – Jacobinism – together with the stirrings of Home rule agitation provided discussions, reports and comments to give the reader a balanced view of 'The Irish Problem'.

Detailed accounts of Irish history and society were printed from *Ireland, Statistical and Political*, by Edward Wakefield (1812), in October 1813. The 'historical background' mentioned the treatment of peasants as worse than in African colonies and India. The term 'moral degradation' appeared a number of times. Quoting sources which included the *Edinburgh Review* and the novelist Maria Edgeworth, the causes were said to be: the prevalence of 'Popish' religion and cruelty against the Catholics, the want of schools and parish churches, absenteeism of the clergy and landlords and the oppression of the poor by middle-men who bought up land, dispossessed tenants, reduced wages and raised prices.

General ignorance on the subject of Ireland (and of the poor Irish) was such that Irish MPs were urged to act for the improvement of conditions by, for example, legislating for schools like the British and Lancaster Schools in England.

Until Catholic Emancipation in 1829, most of the Irish population was unrepresented in Parliament. Their cause was promoted by organisations like the Irish Catholic Association, and 'disturbances' through Dublin and rural Ireland were frequent, together with attacks on Protestants, and an assassination attempt on the Viceroy, Marquess Wellesley, in January 1823.

Irish regiments had fought with distinction throughout the Napoleonic Wars, for example the Royal Dublin Fusiliers at Waterloo, and the bravery of the Irish in both the army and navy was noted. Irish navvies had dug the English canals, but it was the large numbers of Irish emigrants to the mainland, taking jobs in factories of the north and in Scotland, but living in poverty and squalor which offended their English contemporaries. Subscriptions from the general public for the relief of Irish distress were frequent and a meeting in Windsor Town Hall to aid the problem was reported on 28 May 1823.

After many years, and with accompanying newspaper coverage, Daniel O'Connell became the first Catholic MP taking his seat in Parliament in 1830, for County Clare, but the battle for Home Rule increased throughout the century, as did Irish immigration to the British mainland.

There were problems on the mainland too, especially after Waterloo, when armies no longer placed orders for goods. Unemployment increased and the price of bread rose. Refractory cotton spinners, weavers and miners, without representation in Parliament and meeting to express their grievances, alarmed the authorities. Fearing riots and in the absence of a police force the militia was sent to restore and maintain order. On 16 August 1819 between 50 and 80 thousand unarmed radicals marched to St Peter's Fields, Manchester to hear the renowned 'Orator' Henry Hunt. The Yeomanry sent to arrest him panicked, drew their sabres, and slashing through the crowd killed 10 and injured 500. This, known as the Peterloo Massacre, was fully reported, together with Hunt's arrest and later trial for sedition. Windsor readers would probably have agreed with the editor's comment that 'we happily live in a peaceful agricultural district ... and read with a mixture of terror and astonishment'.

Skilled home-workers having lost their jobs to factories powered by mechanical looms joined the great mass of the unemployed and added to the burden on the parish. And an increased Poor Rate affected middle-class ratepayers, who then tended to raise rents and prices, in addition to reducing wages. Though the *Express* reports frequent instances of philanthropy, distress in the manufacturing districts continued throughout the 1820s with riots by the unemployed, and were suppressed by soldiers. Transgressors when caught were tried and transported.

Agricultural distress was due to poor harvests, the effects of the Enclosure movement, and of the Corn Laws of 1815. Cereal producers were protected against foreign competition and the price of bread increased. In 1829 the Spitalfield weavers protested that the manufacturers of this country were sacrificed to 'satiate a few aristocratic landlords'.

Parliamentary news received detailed attention. Each issue of the paper carried abstracts of important debates of both Houses, and of current legislation. Papers presented to Parliament were summarised, and elections covered in detail, including candidates' addresses and results of voting.

Details of crimes, trials, court proceedings and punishments were widely reported. Repressive legislation, brought about from fears of revolution, increased immediately after the peace, but by 1830 such fears had eased, though crimes such as murders and poaching offences continued to be reported and made interesting, if ghoulish reading. The exploits of Burke and Hare were reported in 1828 (they committed murders in order to sell the corpses for dissection), and an account (7 February 1829) of William Burke's execution. By poetic justice Burke was himself dissected afterwards and the paper included a piece on his 'phrenological development' (the study of the skull for what they believed it could tell of behavioural tendencies). William Hare had turned King's evidence and was released.

Regular features on economic, social and cultural events, together with science and technology informed readers on topics of finance, with news of banks, the funds, dividends, bankruptcies, trade and agriculture, with commodity and crop prices and news of harvests.

Archaeology and antiquities were topics stimulated by the Grand Tour of the previous century, and the work of the French in excavating North African sites. In 1816 the paper had news of excavations at Herculaneum, and about the ruins at Carthage. An Egyptian mummy from Thebes was presented to the Newcastle Philosophical Society in October 1821, and an Egyptian obelisk arrived at Deptford in the same month.

A column on literature was regularly included, sometimes noting new books and poetry and including a review or extract from one of the quality journals. A review of *Kenilworth,* by the author of *Waverley* and a notice of the forthcoming *The Monastery*, appeared on 21 January 1821, taken from *Blackwood's Magazine* (Walter Scott's early novels were published anonymously). Also in 1821 was a review of Maria Edgeworth's *Prudence and Principle* which, in an age when novels were dubiously regarded, 'we can safely recommend ... to the most fastidious as a valuable addition to the libraries of young persons which often do as much mischief in small towns among one sex as the alehouses do among the other'. This was Charles Knight's comment. The Knights ran a small circulating library in their shop on Castle Hill, in addition to selling books and tracts which they advertised on the front page of the *Express*.

Under the heading *Magazine Day*, journals such as the *Edinburgh Magazine*, *London Magazine*, *New Monthly* and *European Magazine* were regularly quoted, and closer to home *The Etonian* was reviewed with some poems and extracts of articles (29 June 1824).

Improvements in travel and transport were frequently noted, from turnpike roads in a report of 8 November 1818, and coach journeys between London and the Provinces. In 1821 the Manchester Express at a speed of 10-11 mph left London at 4pm, arriving in Manchester at 11am next day. The construction of new bridges – over the Forth (30 August 1818) and London Bridge with the deepest foundations for coffer dams (6 January 1827) cut down on distances when coaches could cross rivers. News of 'the much-talked scheme to cut a canal across the Isthmus of Suez' appeared on 17 January 1829, which had implications for trade and Empire (but it would not be completed for another 50 years).

Readers would have been aware of the steam engine and its use in the mining and quarrying districts to carry loads. Throughout the 1820s this new invention was developed culminating in the first railways and steam trains. The opening of the Manchester and Liverpool Railway was fully reported (18 September 1830), with a description of the journey and attitude of the crowds as a breach of the peace was feared. Opposing views were presented, on the one hand 'there was too much of the showman about it to please taste', and on the other, approval of a 'work of substantial utility'. But there was a low point to the occasion: the tragic accident that caused the death of the MP William Huskisson. 'Dreadful accident to and death of Mr Huskisson' announced the *Express*, taking the news 'from last night's *Courier*'. Following this setback to railway development there were reports and comments on their effect. The London press was blamed for not exposing the 'villainy of railroads' (16 October 1830), and there were frequent accidents reported with wheels falling off, engines thrown off tracks and people injured. Nothing would stop the development of rail travel, however, though it would be nearly twenty years before Windsor got its own service.

Express editors kept Windsor families well-informed of the world around them. By 1830 the town was on the threshold of an exciting industrial and commercial age, bringing new discoveries, opportunities and social conditions – all of which would be covered by the newspaper, but with new owners and editors. (SS)

The Weather

The newspaper did not carry regular weather reports as we know them today, although it did often report on the state of the harvest, and how it was affected by the weather. From time to time however there were reports of severe weather conditions – storms, floods, snow, ice, and occasionally very hot weather.

The unusual weather during most of 1816, called the 'year without a summer', caused by the eruption of the volcano Tambora in April 1815, is under-reported. Only in November do we find an article on 'the unnatural season of the present year.' The year started with much ice and snow; by the end of April the gooseberries had not bloomed, and there was snow again in May. Then little sunshine and sulphurous clouds, red lightning with unceasing thunder and no gooseberry tarts till July. It was 'the wettest season known, whole fields of corn spoiled'.

Floods

Throughout history, the low-lying areas of Windsor and Eton have suffered from flooding almost every year, the most serious being in 1821. In November 1821, large tracts of the Thames Valley were under water and 'the present floods exceed everything of the kind in the neighbourhood in the last nine years'. The new Windsor Parish church was under construction, and 30 feet of the churchyard wall fell into the High Street following heavy rain. By 29 December 1821 the paper reported:

> The inhabitants of the towns and villages in the vicinity of the Thames are driven for shelter to the upper rooms of their houses; the communication between one place and another is cut off except by means of boats; the roads and bridges are in many places blown up and business is entirely suspended. From Windsor Terrace and other heights, there is nothing to be seen but an awful expanse of waters, the hedges in many places scarcely peeping above the dreary level, and here and there an insulated cottage calling up the most pitying reflections of the wretchedness of its lonely inmates.

The flood began in Eton on Christmas Day. During the following 12 hours the water rose by an astonishing height of two feet. Many of the farmers have 'sustained the most severe losses by the floods penetrating to their barns and corn-stacks'. By 5 January 1822, the flood had started to recede, and the weather was very mild, with early spring flowers, but the misery of local people in low-lying areas continued:

> Those who would know what personal suffering is should seek out the dwellings of the poor, where the visitation is most severely felt. Families have been driven from their sitting rooms to their upper apartments, where in most cases there is no means of procuring a fire; all their comforts are destroyed; they creep about in the waters with the hope of recovering something from the wreck, or sit in wretched inaction amidst the damps with which they are surrounded.

Yet again in November 1823, there was a scene of 'complete inundation' with snow and rain falling for several days. Every road to Datchet was impassable and coaches to London were obliged to proceed up the Long Walk and through Egham. Eton was almost totally under water.

Such frequent flooding had an effect on the infrastructure, especially on the approach to Windsor from the west:

> The entrance to the town of Windsor, by Clewer Lane, (now Oxford Road) is so notoriously bad, as to be a disgrace to the town, and a public nuisance; and the whole of the approach from Clewer is highly objectionable, not only from the contracted width, which is really dangerous at all times, but also from its lying so low as to be wholly impassable during the Thames floods.

A new road was suggested and planned on higher ground to the south, to avoid the annual flooding and this became Clarence Road.

In December 1827, the building of the town's new gasworks in The Goswells had to be suspended because the site was under water. Clewer Lane was once again impassable because of two to three feet of water, and the Home Park had the appearance of a peaceful lake, adorned with rows of magnificent trees.

Heavy rain and floods were not restricted to the winter, and they presented a particular hazard to young children living near the river. In one week in June 1824, two boys were drowned, one at the end of Bier Lane (River Street) and one at Black Potts. In that same week, the Royal Horse Guards marched out of Windsor 'during the most pitiless storm of rain'.

Any accompanying lightning was described using the language of the time, as in July 1826, when after a day of storms with some hailstones 'as big as pigeons' eggs,' the malt-house of The Christopher Inn at Eton, in the occupation of Messrs Ramsbottom and Legh, was struck by the 'electric fluid'. It passed through the window and wall of the upper room, ripping the roof and tearing down the plaster in its escape. In its descent, it split the handle of a malt shovel, as well as a carriage stretcher. The adjacent house of Mrs Valancy was also struck, and the 'fluid having penetrated the wall, passed by a bell-wire through the premises, tearing up the papering of the rooms in its passage'.

In November 1825, violent storms uprooted trees in Windsor Great Park and the Royal Standard was torn from its staff on the Round Tower. Other mentions of lightning were in August 1821, when an oak tree was destroyed at Spital, and in August 1827 a working ox belonging to the King was killed in Windsor Great Park.

Snow and Ice.

Another winter hazard was snow and ice. The start of January 1814 was particularly severe:

> that part of the river below Windsor Bridge called Mill River has been frozen over, and has been crowded with persons partaking in the diversions of skating etc. A singular, though dangerous contrivance of some bargeman excited much attention. A strong pole was fixed in the ice, round which, at a few feet distant, a coach wheel was made to revolve, being driven along by men. From the centre of this wheel issued a rope, at the end of which was a box, in which the person desirous of a whirl was seated. As the wheel revolved, the box described

a circle of about 90 yards, with astonishing velocity, going nearly at the rate of a mile a minute.

Unsurprisingly there were accidents, several people were badly bruised and the merry-go-round had to be stopped. One week later, the wind had shifted to the south-west, and a thaw ensued.

After Princess Augusta moved to Frogmore in 1818, she would give permission for the frozen lake at Frogmore to be opened to the public for skating.

A report in December 1820 described the Thames at Windsor Bridge as almost frozen across, and once again the Mill River was completely frozen and presented an animated scene of skaters.

It was well known that the worst floods often followed prolonged freezes, and during the January 1814 freeze described above, the newspaper had warned:

> All persons who are liable to be injured or incommoded by the overflowing of the Thames or other rivers would do well to prepare for a very high flood on the breaking up of the present frost... Should the thaw be sudden, and accompanied with much rain, a tremendous inundation may be expected, as the whole will precipitate itself into the rivers.

There was still snow on the ground in March 1814, which helped to catch a thief. Mr Marshall the nurseryman and Mr Bedborough the stonemason had a wheelbarrow and other items stolen from their premises, and were able to follow tracks in the snow to an obscure passage in Park Street, where they recovered their goods and other items previously stolen in the town. (SA)

And Finally...

A Kite-drawn vehicle

In August 1826, an eccentric form of transport was spotted passing through Reading on the road from Bristol to London. A light four-wheel carriage carrying three passengers was drawn by two kites. The large main kite was twenty feet high and 170 feet from the ground, with a smaller pilot kite a further 170 feet up. A drum underneath the carriage was used to wind the cord of the pilot kite, or let it out, to avoid roadside hazards such as trees, and the main kite was made of cambric muslin covered in tissue paper and painted to resemble a balloon. The owner, Mr Pocock, a mathematics teacher from Bristol, claimed a speed of 18-20 mph. Indeed some horse-drawn vehicles which attempted to accompany him were unable to keep up, and the kite-drawn vehicle was able to match the speed of the galloping horses pulling the Duke of Gloucester's carriage.

In Reading, to avoid the steeple of St Giles's church, Mr Pocock disengaged the cord from the carriage, and about six men took it round the steeple before re-attaching it. The kites were so powerful that the men were almost lifted off their feet.

> A phenomenon occurred on Saturday the 23d ult. between 10 and 11 o'clock, at Lambourn, Berks. A medical gentleman and his servant were returning home, and were startled by a sudden and brilliant light, which rapidly crossed the heavens from south to north, and appeared to lose itself in the north, but not to decline towards the earth. When the light disappeared, a violent rumbling noise was heard from the north, and appeared to diverge to the east and west, like the bursting of a large cannon. The noise exceeded thunder, and continued nearly five minutes. The heavens were beautifully clear and starlight, both before and after this occurrence. The phenomenon was witnessed by several persons in Oxford.

1823

Daily Shopping

Where did the ordinary citizens of Windsor shop for their basic foodstuffs and other supplies? The 1810 map of the town centre shows that the houses were crowded together on both sides of Thames Street (including around the Castle), Bier Lane, George Street and Peascod Street. Many of these were shops as well as homes.

There were almost 20 bakers, 15 butchers and about 30 grocers, cheesemongers and tea dealers. Fruit and vegetables were grown in gardens, orchards and farmland to the south and west of the town centre. In addition, there were markets in the Corn Exchange and High Street on Wednesdays and Saturdays where the residents were abundantly supplied with 'every article of luxury and necessary (sic) of life'. (SA)

Windsor and Eton Express, AND GENERAL ADVERTISER,

OF THE COUNTIES OF

BERKS, BUCKS, MIDDLESEX, SURRY, HERTS, OXON, HANTS, AND WILTS.

Published at WINDSOR, on SATURDAY EVENING; and distributed within a Circuit of Thirty Miles, early on Sunday Morning.

| No. 1.] | SATURDAY, AUGUST 1, 1812. | [Price Sixpence-Halfpenny |

Data base

1 Aug

p.1   Publishers' statement of intent. The Willows to let for 7 years, truly comfortable house, neatly furnished, 15 acres of land.

p.2   James Hakewill's book *An Historical and Picturesque Description of Windsor* advertised.

p.3   Parliament, debate on state of the nation and renewal of the war in the north of Europe.

p.4   Weekly health bulletin of George III, also weekly outings etc of members of the royal family.

Theatre Royal Windsor opened for the summer season by John O'Keefe, with celebrated comedy *Wild Oats*. [This play was successfully revived in London in the 1970s.]

Sermon preached in Windsor Parish Church on the Bible Society.

Officer of 23rd Light Dragoons rode his horse up 142 steps of the '100 steps' to the Cloisters.

Post-boy sent to gaol for 14 days for letting a man ride on post-horse which carried mailbag for Staines.

8 Aug

p.1   State lottery to be drawn on 8 Sept, prizes between £22 and £16,000.

p.2   'Glorious victory' in Spain, French army routed near Salamanca by allied army under Lord Wellington.

p.3   A shark of considerable length, caught near Plymouth, had attacked a soldier and severely lacerated his legs.

p.4   Revival of royal promenade in Long Walk; the band of 29th Regiment entertained the 'brilliant company'.

Theatre review; *Macbeth, The Sons of Erin, Darkness Visible* and *How to Die for Love*, were performed. Birthday ball for Prince Regent, band of 29th Regiment will play. 29th Regiment in Windsor.

Messrs Trigg and Son of Eton get contract to build a gallery in the north aisle of the Parish church for £358.

15 Aug

p.1   Gentleman will take into his family a limited number of pupils for religious and moral instruction, at 70 guineas per annum, including washing.

p.2   Paris, bulletin of the progress of Napoleon's Grand Army into Russia.

p.3   The Vaccination Establishment is in favour of the new inoculation against smallpox; mortality has dropped from 2,000 last year to 751 in nine London areas where vaccination was introduced.

p.4   Confirmation of Wellington's victory in Portugal.

Prince Regent's birthday celebrations at Frogmore, the Queen's and Prince Regent's bands played. 40 Charity children of Her Majesty's school will dine in tents in Frogmore. Theatre Royal, Mrs Jane Powell to play the prince in *Hamlet*.

22 Aug

p.1   Old established Public House, King's Arms near Windsor Bridge, to be let.

p.p.2-3 List of wounded, missing and killed at Battle of Salamanca.

p.3   Regiments of Life Guards, the Blues, Coldstream Guards and 59th Regiment ready for service in Spain.

p.4   Windsor illuminations to celebrate victory over the French.
        29th Regiment fire gun salute at Frogmore.Prince Regent reviewed his regiment, the 23rd of Foot, on Hounslow Heath.Review of Mrs Powell at Theatre Royal – difficult part, admirably sustained.

29 Aug

p.1   For sale by Daniel Smith, household furniture of Stephen Round, leaving his residence in Peascod St.

p.2   Prince Regent grants coat of arms to Arthur Wellesley, in recognition of victory at Salamanca.

p.3   Riots in Sheffield over price of flour, the Riot Act was read and 'the military put in motion'.

p.4   Royal Review of 23rd Light Dragoons on Hounslow Heath.
        Mr Simms, gardener of Eton College, was robbed of his best stock of fruit and vegetables.
        Lord Harcourt gave splendid ball to nobility and gentry at St Leonard's Hill.
        A man drove a wheel from Hyde Park Corner to Windsor and back in eight hours for a wager.

5 Sep

p.1   New publications include *Rowlin's Complete Cow Doctor,* price 2s 6d and *The Windsor Guide* price 2s.

p.2   *Political Inquirer* examines Parliamentary reform.

p.3   River pirates at Battersea, Mr Geoffrey was mugged by three ruffians while sailing on the Thames.

p.4   New Royal Military College at Sandhurst will assemble on 19 October.
        Prince Regent is to adopt Windsor as his favoured residence. Major Jane and Mr Forman fought a duel on Bagshot Heath; dispute about a lady at Egham race ball. They fired twice but no one was hurt.

12 Sep

p.1   Returns of killed, wounded and missing and of prisoners of war after recent engagements in the Peninsular.
        Enclosure notice for Windsor Forest.

p.2   From the French papers, bulletins of the Grand Army on their victorious march to Moscow.

p.3   News from America, report on Anglo–American hostilities.

p.4   Earl of Harrington, Governor of Windsor Castle, entertained General Forbes and the officers of the 29th to dinner in the Round Tower.
        Ann Cockford of Clewer was fined one guinea for stealing railings from an inclosure in the Goswells.

19 Sep

p.1   Threat of prosecution of anyone found shooting game in the forest.
       Maidenhead turnpike tolls to be let.

p.2   *Political Inquire*r on the reform of the Sicilian constitution.

p.3   Chronological table of events of the Peninsular Campaign 1806-1812.

p.4   The editor is happy to contradict rumours that King George III has experienced
       another severe paroxysm. Price of bread 20d a quartern loaf.

26 Sep

p.1   Address to electors of the borough of Windsor by Edward Disbrowe and John
       Ramsbottom.

p.2   *Political Inquirer*: more on the war with America; to be continued.

p.3   Old Bailey, on Monday 6 prisoners were sentenced to death including M Rogers for
       uttering a counterfeit shilling, having been convicted of a similar
       offence, and Pietro Poloni for stealing clothes.

p.4   Affray between market gardener of Windsor and 3 soldiers of the 39th Regiment, who
       had been stripping fruit from his garden. One soldier was shot in the hand. They will be
       tried by military court-martial.
       Inquest on Hannah Cheyney of Clewer who drowned herself in the Thames.
       Verdict: lunacy.

3 Oct 1812

p.1   New state lottery, 1,950 prizes between £20,000 and £22. Tickets and shares from C
       Knight and Son.

p.2   *Political Inquirer* looks at America's declaration of war against Britain.

p.3   Ceremony at Whitehall Chapel of depositing French eagles 'heroically wrested from
       French'.

p.4   Terrace ghost: soldier on sentry thought he had seen a ghost in the guardroom in an
       agitated state, the sweat running off his face'. Explained as optical illusion 'played off
       from an adjacent window'.
       2 guineas reward for return of black gelding, lost out of the Lammas; if stolen, 5 pounds
       on conviction.

10 Oct

p.1   British Fire Insurance Office, Windsor agent C Knight.

p.2   Account of the Battle of Borodino and occupation of Moscow by Napoleon.

p.3   Violent earthquake on 11 September in Florence destroyed church of St Quirino.

p.4   John Snowden was sworn into office as Mayor of Windsor,
       Dinner at Town Hall included officers of 29th Regiment.
       Windsor election, Edward Disbrowe and John Ramsbottom stand; Electors reminded of
       their duty.
       The blacksmith's shop of John Allen at Datchet burnt down.

17 Oct

p.1   R Lewis, real hat-maker and hosier, Eton, hats cleaned, dyed or altered.

p.2   Reports from Moscow, St Petersburg and Paris on the French assault on Russia, many
       dead and wounded at the Battle of Borodino, [French lost 40,000]; city of Moscow set
       alight.

p.3   Reopening of Drury Lane Theatre after destruction by fire in 1809.

p.4   The Queen and Princesses Elizabeth and Mary inspected their Female School of
       Industry in Old Windsor.

Four troops of Royal Horse Guards the Blues [RHG] return to Windsor and four troops go to Lisbon.

House of Major Bull near Beaconsfield consumed by fire.

24 Oct

p.1 Regulations concerning gathering of dead wood in Windsor Great Park.

Horses taken in to winter at Old Windsor; warm yards, good water and careful persons at Manor Farm.

p.2 Dreadful tornado in New Orleans in September, of 60 vessels in the harbour only one was saved.

p.3 Two French prisoners were returned to France, the officer to be exchanged for a British officer of equal rank.

p.4 Death of Dr James Lind, FRS aged 77, who practised as a physician in Windsor for over 30 years. [He lived at the Limes.]

The Windsor fair was unusually well attended, 'cattle went off briskly, especially heifers and yearlings'.

Price of bread 18½ d after good harvest.

31 Oct

p.1 Return of killed and wounded at the siege of the castle of Burgos in Spain.

p.2 New regulations for Windsor Great Park to stop 'depredations committed' to trees and plantations by 'men women and children who have now indiscriminate access to every part of it'.

p.3 Man was bled twice after a bite from a mad dog and showed signs of rabies, but was cured!

p.4 Robbery at the Three Tuns PH; thief who had paid for his lodgings took the curtains of the bed.

The Royal Military College has moved from Marlow to Sandhurst.

Large gang of pickpockets at Marlow Fair. One man lost £50, another £30, only one was apprehended.

7 Nov 1812

p.1 Regency Eating House to open in Thames Street, hot joints of meat every day.

p.2 Old Bailey: Two men were capitally indicted for stealing 10 bales of silk and two boxes of feathers on the Thames.

p.3 Madrid: English officers have given daily dinners to about 200 starving local people, some persons of high distinction, who would otherwise have perished.

p.4 The King has not been well for the last few days, as for some time previous. The 20th anniversary of the Windsor Club celebrated at the Castle Inn, Windsor MP E Disbrowe in chair.

This is a sample of the Database which was prepared while writing this book. The whole file for the period 1812-1830 will be available shortly on www.TheRoyalWindsorWebsite.com and the Windsor Local History Group's website www.windlesora.org.uk. Additional years will be added later.